EDWARD ALBEE

TWENTIETH CENTURY VIEWS

The aim of this series is to present the best in contemporary critical opinion on major authors, providing a twentieth century perspective on their changing status in an era of profound revaluation.

Maynard Mack, *Series Editor*
Yale University

EDWARD ALBEE

A COLLECTION OF CRITICAL ESSAYS

Edited by

C. W. E. Bigsby

Prentice-Hall, Inc. A SPECTRUM BOOK *Englewood Cliffs, N.J.*

Library of Congress Cataloging in Publication Data

BIGSBY, C W   E
  Edward Albee: a collection of critical essays.

  (Twentieth century views) (A Spectrum Book)
  Bibliography: p.
  CONTENTS: Weales, G. Edward Albee: don't make
waves.—Esslin, M. The Theatre of the Absurd: Edward
Albee—Way, B. Albee and the Absurd: The American
dream and The zoo story. [etc.]
    1. Albee, Edward, 1928–   —Criticism and
interpretation—Addresses, essays, lectures.
PS3551.L25Z583   812'.5'4   74–30464
ISBN 0–13–021311–X
ISBN 0–13–021303–9 pbk.

10 9 8 7 6 5 4 3 2 1

PRENTICE-HALL INTERNATIONAL, INC. (*London*)
PRENTICE-HALL OF AUSTRALIA, PTY. LTD. (*Sydney*)
PRENTICE-HALL OF CANADA, LTD. (*Toronto*)
PRENTICE-HALL OF INDIA PRIVATE LIMITED (*New Delhi*)
PRENTICE-HALL OF JAPAN, INC. (*Tokyo*)

For Jordan and Elaine Miller

Acknowledgments

Quotations from *The Death of Bessie Smith* by Edward Albee are used by kind permission of Coward, McCann & Geoghegan, Inc., Jonathan Cape Ltd, and the author. Copyright © 1960 by Edward Albee.

Quotations from *The Zoo Story* by Edward Albee are used by kind permission of Coward, McCann & Geoghegan, Inc., Jonathan Cape Ltd, and the author. Copyright © 1960 by Edward Albee.

Quotations from *The American Dream* by Edward Albee are used by kind permission of Coward, McCann & Geoghegan, Inc., Jonathan Cape Ltd, and the author. Copyright © 1960, 1961 by Edward Albee.

Quotations from *The Ballad of the Sad Café* by Carson McCullers and Edward Albee are used by kind permission of Houghton Mifflin Company, The Lantz Office, Incorporated, and William Morris Agency.

Quotations from *Box and Quotations from Chairman Mao-Tse Tung* by Edward Albee are used by kind permission of Atheneum Publishers, Jonathan Cape Ltd, and the author. Copyright © 1969 by Edward Albee.

Quotations from *A Delicate Balance* by Edward Albee are used by kind permission of Atheneum Publishers, Jonathan Cape Ltd, and the author. Copyright © 1966 by Edward Albee.

Contents

Introduction

by C. W. E. Bigsby

It is, perhaps, a little uncharitable to begin a book of this kind by deploring some aspects of drama criticism in America. But it is not, in fact, inappropriate that a collection of essays on the work of Edward Albee should begin in such a way. Few playwrights can have been so frequently and mischievously misunderstood, misrepresented, overpraised, denigrated, and precipitately dismissed. Canonized after the performance of his first play, *The Zoo Story,* he found himself in swift succession billed as America's most promising playwright, leading dramatist, and then, with astonishing suddenness, a "one-hit" writer with nothing to his credit but an ersatz masterpiece patched together from the achievements of other writers. The progression was essentially that suggested by George in *Who's Afraid of Virginia Woolf?,* "better, best, bested."

The distinction between a critic and a reviewer is a real one and yet one which few feel any obligation to sustain. The George Jean Nathan Award for Dramatic Criticism is awarded, unblushingly, to what are in fact theatre reviews culled from weekly journals. Reviews are frequently reprinted in book form with no apparent effort to revise the curious blend of whimsy and rhetoric evidently thought appropriate to weekly journalism and with little or no attempt to augment or reconsider the instant opinions which are, unavoidably, the reviewer's stock in trade. Constrained by necessary limitations as to space and influenced, on occasion, by the nature of weekly journalism into an abrasiveness which is too often regarded as the mark of a distinctive critical personality, the reviewer at times embraces an arbitrary "thumbs up/thumbs down" mentality of astounding presumptuousness. The risk then is that the work of a dramatist such as Albee may prove little more than good copy for the drama editor or the pretext for campaigns of a broader nature, theatrical and otherwise, by the reviewer. Even Robert Brustein, one of America's best theatrical observers and a man more aware than most of the limitations of the field in which he works, is not immune to such temptations. Thus, in a review of *The Zoo Story*, later reprinted in *Seasons of Discontent*, he coyly hints at a "masochistic-homosexual perfume" [1] which he forebears to elaborate, and uses the play as a weapon to belabor Allan Ginsberg and, somewhat more strangely, Luce publications. Similarly, in approaching *The American Dream* and *The Death of Bessie Smith* he evidently feels only the slightest obligation to discuss the plays, preferring, once again, to attack *Time* magazine and the general decadence of American theatre. The consequence is, I regret, a casually dismissive attitude which substitutes challenging generalizations for a sensitive response to individual plays.[2]

Nor is the academic world much better. To read the bulk of criticism that Albee's work has inspired is to discover the depths to which abstruse pedantry and the Ph.D. industry can go. And, worse still, a number of sizable red-herrings have been dragged across the path of audience and reader alike by those who wish to see his work as an expression of a particular dramatic movement or pathological condition. Thus, when Martin Esslin chose to discuss Albee in the context of the theatre of the absurd and even included *The Zoo Story* in a collection with the title *Absurd Drama,* he precipitated a host of articles in which Albee was alternately praised and denounced for his success or failure in adopting an approach to which he was at best distantly related. Meanwhile, Philip Roth and others have repeatedly, and irrelevantly, assailed him for writing thinly-veiled homosexual fantasies, *The Zoo Story* being dismissed as an image of pederastic contact, and *Who's Afraid of Virginia Woolf?* as a play originally written for four men. Roth's review of *Tiny Alice* was entitled, "The Play that Dare Not Speak Its Name." [3]

Richard Schechner, the editor of the prestigious *Tulane Drama Review*, hinted at a similar preoccupation in a curiously perverse attack which he chose to launch on *Who's Afraid of Virginia Woolf?* Schechner's violent denunciation is the more surprising and disturbing given the reputation of TDR. He dismissed Albee's first three-act play for its "dirty jokes . . . Self-pity, drooling, womb-seeking weakness"

1 Robert Brustein, *Seasons of Discontent: Dramatic Opinions 1959–1965* (London: Jonathan Cape Ltd., 1966), p. 29.

2 The reviews reprinted in the following pages, offering as they do, an immediate response to individual productions, are intended to complement the fuller critical discussions which follow them.

3 Philip Roth, "The Play that Dare Not Speak Its Name," *New York Review of Books,* iv (February 25, 1965), 4. See p. 105 in this volume.

and for its "persistent escape into morbid fantasy." He drew attention to what he regarded as its "morbidity and sexual perversity which are there only to titillate an impotent and homosexual theatre and audience."

The problem is not so much that he has completely misunderstood the play (seeing "an ineluctable urge to escape reality and its concomitant responsibilities by crawling back into the womb, or bathroom, or both" where the play actually urges the exact opposite) as that, in identifying what he takes to be "bad taste, morbidity, plotless naturalism, misrepresentation of history, American society, philosophy and psychology," he sets himself not to a close examination of the play's vices and virtues but to a denunciation of Albee as a "plague in our midst" and a "corrosive influence on our theatre." [4] The tone is familiar from the early English reviews of Ibsen's work and the parallel is not entirely inappropriate, for Albee, like Ibsen, has all too often been attacked for reasons which have only a passing relevance to his achievements as a dramatist. When *Who's Afraid of Virginia Woolf?* was nominated for the Pulitzer Prize by the drama sub-committee, the nomination was rejected on the ground that, as one member of the full committee remarked, "it was a filthy play." [5] In the end no award was made that year. Typically, the committee subsequently relented by awarding the much inferior *A Delicate Balance* the prize which should have gone to the earlier play.

So what are we to make of a playwright so swiftly granted the accolade of major dramatist and so promptly stripped of his laurels when he failed to produce the string of popular and critical successes which his early work had seemed to promise? What genuinely are his virtues and vices? Why was his work accorded such instant recognition and why has he suffered a decline in reputation in recent years?

The answer lies partly in the condition of American theatre in 1959, the year of *The Zoo Story*. Broadway had suffered a marked decline over a period of years. In 1929 there were seventy-five theatres used for legitimate productions in New York City; by 1959 the figure was down to thirty-three. In 1929 there were two hundred and thirty-three new productions; in 1959 only fifty-six, relatively few of the nonmusical productions being American. Over the same period costs had increased

[4] Richard Schechner, "TDR Comment," *Tulane Drama Review*, VII, iii (Spring, 1963), 8–10. Schechner's article is reprinted in this volume.

[5] Quoted in Wendell V. Harris, "Morality, Absurdity, and Albee," *Southwest Review*, XXIX, iii (Summer, 1964), 249.

between six and eight-fold.[6] To many people the American theatre
seemed threatened with imminent collapse, while the great dramatists
who had sustaind the international reputation of American drama for
so long were no longer in evidence. O'Neill was dead. And, one is
tempted to say, finally and irrevocably dead, for the posthumous
production of his last plays seemed finally ended with *A Touch of the
Poet* in 1958. Arthur Miller seemed to have lost interest in the theatre.
His last play, *A View from the Bridge,* had appeared in 1955 and
his next was not to be produced until 1964. And, finally, Tennessee
Williams had entered a period of decline during which his plays increasingly seemed to be little more than parodies of his own earlier
work. So, the situation was desperate, and America was looking with
some urgency for a new dramatist in whom it could place its faith. It
was clear that that writer would not appear on a Broadway which was
scarcely renowned for its fearless support of new writers dedicated to
extending the boundaries of theatre. Thus it was that attention turned
to Off-Broadway and in particular to writers like Jack Gelber, Jack
Richardson, Arthur Kopit, and Edward Albee, who were hailed in
somewhat extravagant terms when they first appeared. For they were
not merely new American dramatists; they were young men charged
with the responsibility of rescuing the American theatre.

The revival of Off-Broadway had started in the early fifties, the
number of productions expanding from six, in 1950, to seventy-four, in
1959. Not all of these were new or challenging plays. Indeed, the production of original American plays was itself something of an innova-
tion since these small groups usually made their reputations with
productions of European classics or with revivals of early O'Neill, or
Williams. In 1959, however, with the Living Theatre's production of
Jack Gelber's *The Connection* and the European production of Albee's
The Zoo Story (produced Off-Broadway in the following year), we
witnessed what were simply the two best first plays ever written by
American dramatists. The excitement was, therefore, wholly explicable.
And while it was true that if they had not existed they would have
had to be invented (witness Brustein's subsequent desperate effort to
elevate the undergraduate observations of *MacBird* into a play of real
political and aesthetic significance), it so happened that both brought
qualities to the American theatre which it had patently lacked before.

[6] Statistical information from Jack Poggi, *Theatre in America: The Impact of
Economic Forces: 1870–1967* (Ithaca, N.Y.: Cornell University Press, 1968).

Gelber forged a metaphysical metaphor out of the daily realities of American sub-culture, which was as disturbing theatrically as it was socially. Albee introduced a verbal facility and a dramatic power which one had only glimpsed occasionally in O'Neill's last plays. Gelber's subsequent career was disappointing, as was Kopit's and Richardson's. Only Albee seemed capable of capping the achievement of his early work; only he accomplished the transfer to Broadway and did so without surrendering his commitment to original and challenging drama.

There is no doubt that the Broadway production of *Who's Afraid of Virginia Woolf?* provided the basis for Albee's amazing popular reputation; less obviously, but equally certainly, it was also the primary reason for the suspicion with which some reviewers and critics approached his work. For there was a sense in which the move to Broadway seemed a betrayal of the nascent values of Off-Broadway—a confession that he was a mere entertainer with a talent for simulating seriousness. Certainly the play had originally been intended for production by the Actors Studio, and when Albee urged a Broadway production he was opposed by the play's director. Yet *Who's Afraid of Virginia Woolf?* is by no means conventional Broadway fare. The single claustrophobic set, the excoriating language, the disconcerting emotional and theatrical power, were remote from the usually bland products of the Great White Way. And Albee's decision to use some of the profits from the production to encourage new American dramatists merely underlined his continuing concern with experiment.

The success of *Who's Afraid of Virginia Woolf?* established Albee's reputation around the world, and the curious assaults on the play as epitomizing some presumed decadence either in the state of the American theatre or in his personal sensibility only served to promote considerable interest in him by the media. He became a public figure, lecturing on university campuses and traveling abroad on behalf of the State Department, a curious role for a man whose work has consistently castigated what he sees as a blindly materialistic society devoid of any real sense of values and national purpose. He became, in other words, the Famous American Playwright, whom he had satirized in an early sketch. And now, public and reviewers alike expected him to repeat his early success. His failure to do so led to a curious sense of betrayal in the minds of some people, as the man singled out to take on the burden formerly carried by O'Neill, Miller, and Williams began an

apparently eccentric series of experiments which seemed ill-adapted
to one now widely regarded as a Broadway writer. The truth was that
Albee has remained at heart a product of Off-Broadway, claiming the
same freedom to experiment and, indeed, fail, which is the special
strength of that theatre. The difficulty is that he continues to offer his
plays to a Broadway audience who, even given their tolerance for anything which can be officially ratified as "art," find his refusal to repeat
the formula of *Who's Afraid of Virginia Woolf?* increasingly perverse.
The animus directed at Albee in recent years thus comes, at least in
part, from his failure to realize expectations formed by his first Broadway success as well as, partly, from genuine failures of craft and slack-
ness of artistic control.

What he in fact chose to do was to alternate new works of his own
with adaptations of the work of Carson McCullers, James Purdy, and
Giles Cooper respectively. But while the choice of these particular works
(*The Ballad of the Sad Café, Malcolm, Everything in the Garden*) was
entirely explicable in terms of his own thematic concerns, the decision
to lend his talents to such a project was not. He had early voiced a
suspicion of the whole process of adaptation which has, unfortunately,
proved more than justified by his own efforts in that direction. Carson
McCullers' tortured parable of human relations simply does not bear
a literal translation to the stage, her Gothic images collapsing into
mere pathos as soon as they are objectified. Purdy's "surreal" novel
similarly defies dramatization, the tracery of his baroque imagination
being replaced by ill-judged fantasy and callow sentimentality in a
production which even Albee prefers to forget. Giles Cooper's play,
unremarkable in its original version, gains nothing from Albee's
attempt to Americanize it.

His original plays tell a different story. Though all of them are, I
think, flawed in some important respect, they offer clear evidence of
Albee's commitment to extending his range as a writer. They stand as
proof of his fascination with the nature of theatricality and of his
determination to trace those social and psychological concerns which
have provided the focus for so much American drama to their root in
metaphysical anguish. Tom Driver once said of Arthur Miller that he
lacked "that metaphysical inquisitiveness which would take him to the
bottom of the problems which he encounters" primarily because he
tended to see issues "too soon . . . in their preliminary form of social
or even moral debate" and "not in terms of dramatic events that disturb the audience's idea of basic truth, which is the foundation for

its moral attitudes." [7] Much the same could be said of Tennessee Williams. It is one of Albee's chief virtues as a dramatist that he has revealed precisely that metaphysical inquisitiveness, thereby penetrating—as George says in *Who's Afraid of Virginia Woolf?*—to "the bone . . . the marrow." If he is to be regarded as a social critic, as a number of writers have suggested, then he is what he himself has described as "a demonic social critic," [8] intent on establishing the connection between a collapse of social structure and the failure of nerve on an individual level. And though his work has revealed a considerable stylistic diversity, it is legitimate to talk of his central concerns in this way, for thematically there is a unity to his work which links his first Off-Broadway play to his latest Broadway offering.

His heroes have all failed in some fundamental way. They have betrayed the values to which, even now, they are capable of pledging a belated allegiance. They are liberal humanists who have allowed themselves to become detached from a reality which disturbs them and hence from those individuals who are the expression of their commitment to a vision of private and public responsibility. They have sold out; not for wealth or success, but for an untroubled existence—to preserve their own innocence. Unwilling to recognize that pain is a natural corollary of a free existence, they have blunted their moral convictions with alcohol and a sterile intellectualism, as George has done in *Who's Afraid of Virginia Woolf?*; or they have embraced the spurious consolation offered by religious determinism, as Julian has done in *Tiny Alice;* or they have simply permitted the slow disintegration of human responsibilities, as Tobias has done in *A Delicate Balance.* The consequence of such a drift toward moral extinction is clear enough in the apocalyptic imagery of *Who's Afraid of Virginia Woolf?*, *Box, Quotations from Chairman Mao Tse-Tung,* and *All Over.* The action of the first of these takes place in a town which is pointedly called New Carthage and which is likened to two other cities destroyed by their hedonism and capitalist frenzy, Penguin Island and Gomorrah. The action of the last is concerned with the final collapse of structure in the moment of death.

Albee's work is characterized by an overwhelming sense of loss which, though doubtless rooted in the details of his own painful childhood,

[7] Tom Driver, "Strength and Weakness in Arthur Miller," in *Discussions of American Drama* by Walter Meserve (Boston: D. C. Heath & Company, 1966), p. 110.

[8] Digby Diehl, "Edward Albee Interviewed," *Transatlantic Review,* 13 (Summer, 1963), 72.

becomes an image, firstly, of the loss by America of the principles which had been invoked by its founders, and, secondly, of the inevitable process of deprivation which is the basis of individual existence. The problem which he sets himself is that of formulating a response to this sense of loss which involves neither a self-pitying despair nor capitulation to those facile illusions endorsed by Madison Avenue, the Church, or simply the conventional wisdom of contemporary society. The solution which he advances is essentially a New Testament compassion, a liberal commitment to the Other. That is to say, he attacks a social system which fails in its primary duty of creating a communal responsibility and presents characters who must strip themselves of all pretense if they are to survive as autonomous individuals and accept their responsibility toward other people.

Albee's work is a prophecy and a warning. Nor should the splendid articulateness of the dialogue or the brilliant wit, which is a mark of so many of his plays, be seen as detracting from the seriousness of his diagnosis. For they are themselves a part of the evidence—the means deployed by a sophisticated society to evade the pain of real communication and the menace of a world slipping towards dissolution. Words are used to sustain illusion; laughter to distract and to wound. Albee sets his face resolutely against the "pipe-dreams" endorsed by O'Neill's desperate characters in *The Iceman Cometh* not because he lacks O'Neill's compassion but because he believes that human imperfections and weaknesses must be freely confessed if the individual is ever to make a genuine attempt to establish a necessary relationship with those around him. And if these truths are painful, they are also the only basis on which one can credibly begin the reconstruction of personal and social meaning.

Albee has brought to the theatre not merely a magnificent command of language, a control of rhythm and tone which has never been rivaled in America, but also a sensitivity to dramatic tradition and particularly to the achievements of European dramatists, which gives his work a dimension all too often lacking in American writers. For his part, Robert Brustein chooses to attack much of Albee's work, seeing him merely as an impersonator—a writer of superior pastiche. This is, I think, a curious criticism, for though one can indeed detect in his work elements of Ionesco's style, Strindberg's obsessive misogyny, Eliot's suburban metaphysics, and Miller's liberal *angst*, this is to say no more than that Albee has shown an awareness of the achievement of other writers and a commitment to examining the nature of theatrical experiment. It is surely as much a mistake to regard *Who's Afraid of Virginia Woolf?* as simply a modern version of Strindberg's *A Dance of Death* as it is to see *Tiny Alice* as only a transcribed version of *The Cocktail Party*. The influence is there; the voice is Albee's. The gulf between eclecticism and impersonation is the gulf between honesty and fraud, a receptive imagination and an impoverished sensibility. The Byzantine complexity of *Tiny Alice*, the fascinating blend of strict structure and free form in *Quotations from Chairman Mao Tse-Tung*, and even the misguided attempt to adapt the "surreal" imagination of James Purdy all provide evidence of his refusal to limit his talent . or to accept conventional notions of theatrical propriety. If Albee is not what he seeemd when he first burst upon the scene at the beginning of the sixties, if he was never the absurdist he was taken to be nor the man summoned to redeem Broadway, he was in some ways much more. He was a serious artist with the courage to refuse the blandishments of the commercial theatre. He was a writer who offered genuine gifts, including a mastery of words, a musician's sense of rhythmic structure, an undeniable ability to create dramatic metaphors of compelling power, and, most important of all, a stunning integrity which permits no compromise with his artistic objectives. If this latter has at times led him into misjudgments on a considerable scale, it is also the guarantee that Albee will remain, not merely a dramatist of international reputation, but also, and in ways which early reviewers could not really appreciate, one of the mainstays of American drama over the next decade.

It follows from this that I do not find myself in agreement with all the observations reprinted in the ensuing pages. They do, however, in toto, represent something of the range and variety of opinion which Albee's work has inspired. And if they are not united in approach or even agreed as to Albee's ultimate achievement, they do identify with lucidity and precision the nature and terms of the debate. Where I have chosen to print essays of my own this is because I could find no criticism which emphasized those elements which, for the purposes of this book, I wished to stress.

Edward Albee:
Don't Make Waves

by Gerald Weales

Edward Albee is inescapably *the* American playwright of the 1960's. His first play, *The Zoo Story,* opened in New York, on a double bill with Samuel Beckett's *Krapp's Last Tape,* at the Provincetown Playhouse on January 14, 1960. In his Introduction to *Three Plays* (1960), Albee tells how his play, which was written in 1958, passed from friend to friend, from country to country, from manuscript to tape to production (in Berlin in 1959) before it made its way back to the United States. "It's one of those things a person has to do," says Jerry; "sometimes a person has to go a very long distance out of his way to come back a short distance correctly."

For Albee, once *The Zoo Story* had finished its peregrinations, the trip uptown—psychologically and geographically—was a short one. During 1960, there were two other Albee productions, largely unheralded—*The Sandbox,* which has since become a favorite for amateurs, and *Fam and Yam,* a *bluette,* a joke growing out of his having been ticketed as the latest white hope of the American theater. These were essentially fugitive productions of occasional pieces. In 1961, one of the producers of *The Zoo Story,* Richard Barr, joined by Clinton Wilder in the producing organization that is always called Theater 196? after whatever the year, offered *The American Dream,* first on a double bill with William Flanagan's opera *Bartleby,* for which Albee and James Hinton, Jr., did the libretto,[1] and later, when the opera

"Edward Albee: Don't Make Waves." From Gerald Weales, *The Jumping-Off Place: America Drama in the 1960's* (New York: Macmillan Publishing Co., Inc., 1969), pp. 24–35; 36–39. Copyright © 1969 by Gerald Weales. Reprinted by permission of Macmillan Publishing Co., Inc.

1 According to a letter from Albee (October 13, 1966), Hinton, who was writing the libretto, fell ill and Albee finished the work; as he remembers it, he wrote the Prologue, the last scene, and did "considerable revision" on the other three scenes.

proved unsuccessful, with an earlier Albee play *The Death of Bessie Smith*. During the next few years, there were frequent revivals of both *Zoo* and *Dream*, often to help out a sagging Barr-Wilder program, as in 1964 (by which time Albee had become a co-producer) when first *Dream* and later *Zoo* were sent in as companion pieces to LeRoi Jones's *Dutchman*, after Samuel Beckett's *Play* and Fernando Arrabal's *The Two Executioners*, which opened with Jones's play, were removed from the bill. Albee had become an off-Broadway staple.

By that time, of course, Albee had become something else as well. With *Who's Afraid of Virginia Woolf?* (1962), he had moved to Broadway and had a smashing commercial success. By a process of escalation, he had passed from promising to established playwright. After *Woolf*, Albee productions averaged one a year: *The Ballad of the Sad Café* (1963), *Tiny Alice* (1964), *Malcolm* (1966), *A Delicate Balance* (1966) and *Everything in the Garden* (1967). None of these were successes in Broadway terms (by *Variety's* chart of hits and flops), but except for

---

The title page of the vocal score lists Flanagan with Hinton and Albee as one of the authors of the libretto. The opera, of course, is based on Herman Melville's "Bartleby the Scrivener." My responses are highly suspect since I did not see the opera in production; I read the libretto and listened to at least two of my friends—unfortunately, not at the same time—make piano assaults on the score. I would guess that the most effective scene, musically and dramatically, is Scene 2 in which Mr. Allan (the name given to Melville's nameless lawyer-narrator) goes to his office on Sunday morning and finds Bartleby there; his aria carries him from complacent Sunday-morning ruminations (mostly to slightly doctored lines from Melville) through the confrontation with Bartleby to his attempt to make sense of this clerk who will not do his work and will not go away. Bartleby's one-note "I would prefer not to" echoes in variations all through Allan's confusion in this scene. Less happy moments musically are church bells which chime in the piano part after they have been mentioned in the libretto and the calculated contrast at the end of Scene 3 when beyond the huffing-puffing violence can be heard the soprano of the office boy singing his way back on stage with the ballad-like song that identifies him. For the most part, the libretto is a softening of Melville's story. Since the Bartleby of the story makes a claim on the lawyer which cannot be (or is not) fulfilled, Melville's work has an obvious thematic relevance to Albee's. What is missing in the dramatization is Melville's superb ambiguity; there is not even an attempt in the opera to get the effect that Melville achieves when his narrator, who believes that "the easiest way of life is the best," manages to comfort himself by pigeon-holing Bartleby when the clerk is no longer alive and mutely accusing. The "Oh, Bartleby, Oh, humanity" that ends the opera is sentimental although it probably means to be something more exalted. The "Ah, Bartleby! Ah, humanity!" that ends Melville's story is ironic.

Flanagan, to whom Albee dedicated *The Zoo Story*, did the music for *The Sandbox*, *The Ballad of the Sad Café*, and *Malcolm*. Flanagan's music for *The Sandbox* is printed with the play in Margaret Mayorga's *The Best Short Plays, 1959–1960*.

Malcolm, a gauche and imperceptive adaptation of James Purdy's novel of that name, which closed after seven performances, all of them had respectable runs and generated their share of admiration and antagonism from critics and public alike.

Although favorable reviews helped make the Albee reputation, critics have consistently praised with one hand, damned with the other.[2] If Harold Clurman's "Albee on Balance" (*The New York Times,* January 13, 1967) treats Albee as a serious playwright and if Robert Brustein's "A Third Theater" (*The New York Times Magazine,* September 25, 1966) seems to dismiss him as a solemn one, only Broadway serious, the recent collections of their reviews—Clurman's *The Naked Image* and Brustein's *Seasons of Discontent*—indicate that both critics have had the same kind of reservations about Albee from the beginning. Albee, contrariwise, has had reservations of his own. From his pettish Introduction to *The American Dream* to the press conference he called to chastise the critics for their reactions to *Tiny Alice,* he has regularly used interviews and the occasional nondramatic pieces he has written to suggest that the critics lack understanding, humility, responsibility.

In spite of (perhaps because of) the continuing quarrel between Albee and his critics—a love-hate relationship in the best Albee tradition—the playwright's reputation has grown tremendously. It was in part the notoriety of *Who's Afraid of Virginia Woolf?* that turned Albee into a popular figure, and certainly the publicity surrounding the making of the movie version of *Woolf* helped to keep Albee's name in the popular magazine. Whatever the cause, Albee is now the American playwright whose name has become a touchstone, however ludicrously it is used. Thus, Thomas Meehan, writing an article on "camp" for *The New York Times Magazine* (March 21, 1965), solicits Andy Warhol's opinion of *Tiny Alice* ("I liked it because it was so empty"), and William H. Honan, interviewing Jonathan Miller for the same publication (January 22, 1967), manages to get Miller to repeat a commonplace criticism of Albee he has used twice before.

2 My own reviews, from *The Zoo Story* (*The Reporter,* February 16, 1961) to *Everything in the Garden* (*The Reporter,* December 28, 1967), have suggested with a decreasing amount of flippancy that there is less to Albee than meets the eye. Although my review of *Virginia Woolf* (*Drama Survey,* Fall, 1963) now seems unnecessarily condescending, my general misgivings about Albee as a playwright have not disappeared. What has disappeared, alas, is a letter that Albee sent to *The Reporter* to straighten me out after my review of *The Zoo Story.*

All this is simply the chi-chi mask over a serious concern with Albee. According to recent reports of the American Educational Theatre Association, Albee has been jockeying for second place (after Shakespeare) in the list of playwrights most produced on college campuses. In 1963–64, he held second place; in 1964–65, he was nosed out by Ionesco. The attractiveness of short plays to college dramatic groups—as Ionesco's presence suggests—helps explain the volume of Albee productions, but, with *The Zoo Story* invading text anthologies and *Virginia Woolf* climbing onto reading lists, it is clear that the interest in Albee in colleges is more than a matter of mechanics. More and more articles on Albee turn up in critical quarterlies—always a gauge of academic fashions—and those that are printed are only the tip of a happily submerged iceberg; Walter Meserve, one of the editors of *Modern Drama,* estimated in 1966 that 80 per cent of the submissions on American drama were about four authors: O'Neill, Williams, Miller, and Albee. The interest abroad is as intense as it is here. This is clear not only from the fact that the plays are translated and performed widely, but in the desire of audiences to talk or to hear about the playwright. Clurman, in that article in the *Times,* reporting on lecture audiences in Tokyo and Tel Aviv, says that there was more curiosity about Albee than any other American playwright. Albee's position, then, is analogous to that of Tennessee Williams in the 1950's. He recognizes this himself. When he wrote *Fam and Yam* in 1960, he let Yam (the Young American Playwright) bunch Albee with Jack Gelber, Jack Richardson, and Arthur Kopit. In an interview in *Diplomat* (October, 1966) he suggested that playwrights should be hired as critics; it was now Williams and Arthur Miller that he listed with himself.

In "Which Theatre Is the Absurd One?" (*The New York Times Magazine,* February 25, 1962), Albee wrote that "in the end a public will get what it deserves and no better." If he is right, his work may finally condemn or justify the taste of American theater audiences in the 1960's. More than likely, a little of both.

"I consider myself in a way the most eclectic playwright who ever wrote," Albee once told an interviewer (*Transatlantic Review,* Spring, 1963), and then he went on to make an elaborate joke about how he agreed with the critics that twenty-six playwrights—three of whom he had never read—had influenced him. Critics do have a way of getting influence-happy when they write about Albee—particularly Brustein, who persists in calling him an imitator—but they have good reason. There are such strong surface dissimilarities among the Albee plays that it is easier and in some ways more rewarding to think of *The Zoo Story* in relation to Samuel Beckett and Harold Pinter and *A Delicate Balance* in terms of T. S. Eliot and Enid Bagnold than it is to compare the two plays, even though both start from the same dramatic situation: the invasion (by Jerry, by Harry and Edna) of private territory (Peter's bench, Tobias's house). Yet, the comparison is obvious once it is made. Each new Albee play seems to be an experiment in form, in style (even if it is someone else's style), and yet there is unity in his work as a whole. This is apparent in the devices and the characters that recur, modified according to context, but it is most obvious in the repetition of theme, in the basic assumptions about the human condition that underlie all his work.

In *A Delicate Balance,* Tobias and his family live in a mansion in the suburbs of hell, that existential present so dear to contemporary writers, in which life is measured in terms of loss, love by its failure, contact by its absence. In that hell, there are many mansions—one of which is Peter's bench—and all of them are cages in the great zoo story of life. Peter's bench is a kind of sanctuary, both a refuge from and an extension of the stereotypical upper-middle-class existence (tweeds, horn-rimmed glasses, job in publishing, well-furnished apartment, wife, daughters, cats, parakeets) with which Albee has provided him—a place where he can safely not-live and have his nonbeing. This is the way Jerry sees Peter, at least, and—since the type is conventional enough in contemporary theater, from avant-garde satire to Broadway revue —it is safe to assume that the play does, too. Although Albee intends a little satirical fun at Peter's expense (the early needling scenes are very successful), it is clear that the stereotyping of Peter is an image of his condition, not a cause of it. Jerry, who plays "the old pigeonhole bit" so well, is another, a contrasting cliché, and it is the play's business to show that he and Peter differ only in that he does not share Peter's complacency. Just before Jerry attacks in earnest, he presents the play's chief metaphor:

> I went to the zoo to find out more about the way people exist with animals, and the way animals exist with each other, and with people too. It probably wasn't a fair test, what with everyone separated by bars from everyone else, the animals for the most part from each other, and always the people from the animals. But, if it's a zoo, that's the way it is.

"Private wings," says Malcolm in the play that bears his name. "Indeed, that *is* an extension of separate rooms, is it not?" In a further extension of a joke that is no joke, Agnes, in *A Delicate Balance,* speaks of her "poor parents, in their separate heavens." *Separateness* is the operative word for Albee characters, for, even though his zoo provides suites for two people (*Who's Afraid of Virginia Woolf?*) or for more (*A Delicate Balance*), they are furnished with separate cages. "It's sad to know you've gone through it all, or most of it, without . . ." says Edna in one of the fragmented speeches that characterize *A Delicate Balance,* as though thoughts too were separate, "that the one body you've wrapped your arms around . . . the only skin you've ever known . . . is your own—and that it's dry . . . and not warm." This is a more restrained, a more resigned variation on the Nurse's desperate cry in *Bessie Smith*, ". . . I am tired of my skin. . . . I WANT OUT!"

Violence is one of the ways of trying to get out. The Nurse is an illustration of this possibility; she is an embryonic version of Martha in *Virginia Woolf,* with most of the venom, a little of the style, and practically none of the compensating softness of the later character, and she hits out at everyone around her. Yet, she never escapes herself, her cage. The other possibility is love (that, too, a form of penetration), but the Albee plays are full of characters who cannot (Nick in *Virginia Woolf*) or will not (Tobias, the Nurse) make that connection. The persistent images are of withdrawal, the most graphic being the one in *A Delicate Balance,* the information that Tobias in fact withdrew and came on Agnes's belly the last time they had sex. Although failed sex is a convenient metaphor for the failure of love, its opposite will not work so well. Connection is not necessarily contact, and it is contact —or rather its absence, those bars that bother Jerry—that preoccupies Albee. He lets Martha and George make fun of the lack-of-communication cliché in *Virginia Woolf,* but it is that cultural commonplace on which much of Albee's work is built. Jerry's story about his landlady's vicious dog—although he over-explains it—is still Albee's most effective account of an attempt to get through those bars, out of that skin (so effective, in fact, that Tobias uses a variation of it in *Balance* when he tells about his cat). Accepting the dog's attacks on him as a form of recognition, Jerry tries first to win his affection (with hamburger) and, failing that, to kill him (with poisoned hamburger: it is difficult to differentiate between the tools of love and hate). In the end, he settles for an accommodation, one in which he and the dog ignore each other. His leg remains unbitten, but he feels a sense of loss in the working arrangement: "We neither love nor hurt because we do not try to reach each other." [3]

"Give me *any* person . . ." says Lawyer in *Tiny Alice.* "He'll take what he gets for . . . what he wishes it to be. AH, it is what I have always wanted, he'll say, looking terror and betrayal straight in the eye. Why not: face the inevitable and call it what you have always wanted." The context is a special one here, a reference to Julian's impending martyrdom to God-Alice, who comes to him in the form or forms he expects. I purposely dropped from the Lawyer's speech the references to "martyr" and "saint" which follow parenthetically after the opening phrase, for as it stands above, the speech might serve as advertising copy for the Albee world in which his characters exist and —very occasionally—struggle. The too-obvious symbol of *The American Dream,* the muscle-flexing young man who is only a shell, empty of love or feeling, is, in Mommy's words, "a great deal more like it." *Like it,* but not *it.* Appearance is what she wants, for reality, as Grandma's account of the mutilation of the other "bumble" indicates, is dangerous.

The American Dream is a pat example of, to use Lawyer's words again, "How to come out on top, going under." Whether the accommodation is embraced *(Dream)* or accepted with a sense of loss (Jerry and the dog), it is always there, a way of coping instead of a way of life. It can be disguised in verbal trappings—comic (the games in *Virginia Woolf*) or serious (the religiosity of *Tiny Alice,* the conventional labels of *A Delicate Balance*). In the absence of substance, it can be given

[3] One of the persistent—and, I think, unfortunate—ways of reading Albee is to assume that the animals and the animal imagery which figure in so many of the plays are being used to make some instructive point about man's nature. For instance, John V. Hagopian, in a letter to the *New York Review of Books* (April 8, 1965), insisted that the point of *Tiny Alice* is that "man must embrace his animal nature." It is true that Brother Julian has an abstraction problem in that play, but his acceptance of the world (and all the animals and birds that wander through the lines in *Alice*) is not—as the ambiguity in his death scene indicates—a sure sign of either health or reality. There is a certain amount of sentimentality in such a reading of the play, at least if the "embrace" is taken as positive rather than factual. In Albee's work there is a general equation between man and animal. This can be seen in *The Zoo Story,* not only in Jerry's dog tale and the zoo metaphor, but in the confusion of Peter's children with his cats and parakeets. Perhaps there is something ennobling, an up-the-chain-of-being slogan, in Jerry's comfort to Peter, "you're not really a vegetable; it's all right, you're an animal," but as Mac the Knife would say, "What's the percentage?" Albee's animals reflect the predicament of his men. There are still bars to look through, accommodations to be made.

busy work; Girard Girard spells everything out in *Malcolm:* "You will move from the mansion to the chateau, and from the chateau back. You will surround yourself with your young beauties, and hide your liquor where you will. You will . . . go on, my dear." The unhidden liquor in *A Delicate Balance* (even more in *Virginia Woolf*, where it serves the dramatic action, as lubricant and as occasional rest) provides an example of such busyness: all the playing at bartending, the weighty deliberation over whether to have anisette or cognac, the concern over the quality of a martini. The rush of words (abuse or elegance) and the press of activity (however meaningless) sustain the Albee characters in a tenuous relationship (a delicate balance) among themselves and in the face of the others, the ones outside, and—beyond that—the nameless terror.

Implicit in my discussion of the separateness of the Albee characters and the bogus forms of community they invent to mask the fact that they are alone is the assumption that this is Albee's view of the human condition. The deliberate refusal to locate the action of his most recent plays (*Tiny Alice, Malcolm, A Delicate Balance*) strengthens that assumption. In fact, only two of Albee's settings can be found in atlases —Central Park (*The Zoo Story*) and Memphis (*Bessie Smith*). Even these, like the undifferentiated Southern town he borrowed from Carson McCullers for *The Ballad of the Sad Café* and the fictional New England college town of *Virginia Woolf*, might easily serve as settings for a universal drama. Yet, in much of his work, particularly in the early plays, there is a suggestion, even an insistence, that the problem is a localized one, that the emptiness and loneliness of the characters are somehow the result of a collapse of values in the Western world in general, in the United States in particular. *The American Dream*, he says in his Preface to the play, is "an attack on the substitution of artificial for real values in our society." Such an attack is implicit in the depiction of Peter in *The Zoo Story*.

It is in *Virginia Woolf* that this side of Albee's "truth" is most evident. He is not content that his characters perform an action which carries implications for an audience that far transcend the action itself. He must distribute labels. George may jokingly identify himself, as history professor, with the humanities, and Nick, as biology professor, with science, and turn their meeting into a historical-inevitability parable about the necessary decline of the West, but Albee presumably means it. Calling the town New Carthage and giving George significant throw-away lines ("When I was sixteen and going to prep school, during the Punic Wars . . .") are cute ways of underlining a ponderous intention. I would not go so far as Diana Trilling (*Esquire,* December, 1963) and suggest that George and Martha are the Washingtons, or Henry Hewes (*The Best Plays of 1962–1963*) that Nick is like Nikita Khrushchev, but Albee is plainly intent on giving his sterility tale an obvious cultural point.* Martha's joke when Nick fails to "make it in the sack" is apparently no joke at all: "But that's how it is in a civilized society."

My own tendency is to brush all this grandiose symbol-making under the rug to protect what I admire in *Virginia Woolf.* If we can believe Albee's remarks in the *Diplomat* interview, however, all this comprises the "play's subtleties"; in faulting the movie version of his play, he says, "the entire political argument was taken out, the argument between history and science." [4] The chasm that confronts the Albee characters may, then, be existential chaos or a materialistic society corrupt enough to make a culture hero out of . . . (whom? to each critic his own horrible example, and there are those would pick Albee himself), or a combination in which the second of these is an image of the first.

---

* [Albee has in fact confirmed such an identification in at least two interviews: William Flanagan, "Edward Albee," in *Writers at Work* (London, 1968), p. 338, and Michael E. Rutenberg, *Edward Albee: Playwright in Protest* (New York, 1969), p. 232.—Ed.]

4 Perhaps we cannot believe him. In an article on the making of the movie (*McCall's,* June, 1966), Roy Newquist quotes Albee: "They had filmed the *play,* with the exception of five or ten minutes of relatively unimportant material." Although I quote from a number of interviews in this chapter, I am aware that interviews, at best, are doubtful sources of information and opinion. There are the obvious dangers of misquotation and spur-of-the-moment remarks which are untrue (is *The Ballad of the Sad Café* an earlier play than *Virginia Woolf,* as Albee told Thomas Lask in a *Times* interview, October 27, 1963, or are we to believe the dates accompanying the Atheneum editions of his plays?) or only momentarily true (the conflicting opinions about the movie version of *Woolf*). Beyond that, it is clear that Albee, when he is not on his high horse, likes to kid around. I am not thinking of an occasion like the joint interview with John Gielgud (*Atlantic,* April, 1965), where the chummy inside jocularity masks what must have been a major difference of opinion over *Tiny Alice,* but of an interview like the one in *Transatlantic Review,* in which Albee is very solemn and still sounds as though he is putting Digby Diehl on. Or the one in *Diplomat* that got me into this footnote in the first place, for in that one Albee uses what I assume is a running gag, of which Otis L. Guernsey, Jr., never seems aware. In three variations on a single line, he ponders whether or not *Woolf, Alice,* and *Balance* are comedies on the basis of whether or not the characters get what they want or think they want. The joke, of course, is that the line comes from Grandma's curtain speech from *The American Dream:* "So, let's leave things as they are right now . . . while everybody's happy . . . while everybody's got what he wants . . . or everybody's got what he thinks he wants. Good night, dears."

There is nothing unusual about this slightly unstable mixture of philosophic assumption and social criticism; it can be found in the work of Tennessee Williams and, from quite a different perspective, that of Eugène Ionesco. The differentiation is useful primarily because it provides us with insight into the shape that Albee gives his material. If the lost and lonely Albee character is an irrevocable fact—philosophically, theologically, psychologically—if all that *angst* is inescapable, then his plays must necessarily be reflections of that condition; any gestures of defiance are doomed to failure. If, however, the Albee character is a product of his societal context and if that context is changeable (not necessarily politically, but by an alteration of modes of behavior between one man and another), then the plays may be instructive fables. He has dismissed American drama of the 1930's as propaganda rather than art, and he has disavowed solutions to anything. Still, in several statements he has suggested that there are solutions—or, at least, alternatives. Surely that possibility is implicit in his description of *The American Dream* as an "attack." In the *Transatlantic Review* interview, he said that "the responsibility of the writer is to be a sort of demonic social critic—to present the world and people in it as he sees it and say 'Do you like it? If you don't like it change it.' " In the *Atlantic,* he said, "I've always thought . . . that it was one of the responsibilities of playwrights to show people how they are and what their time is like in the hope that perhaps they'll change it."

Albee, then, shares with most American playwrights an idea of the utility of art, the supposition not only that art should convey truth, but that it should do so to some purpose. There is a strong strain of didacticism in all his work, but it is balanced by a certain ambiguity about the nature of the instructive fable. In interviews, he harps on how much of the creative process is subconscious, how little he understands his own work, how a play is to be experienced rather than understood. Insofar as this is not sour grapes pressed to make an aesthetic (his reaction to the reviews of *Tiny Alice*), it may be his way of recognizing that there is a conflict between his attitude toward man's situation and his suspicion (or hope: certainly *conviction* is too strong a word) that something can, or ought, to be done about it; between his assumption that this is hell we live in and his longing to redecorate it. . . .

It is in *The Zoo Story, Who's Afraid of Virginia Woolf?* and *A Delicate Balance* that one finds dramatic actions by which the ambiguity of Albee's attitudes may be tested. In *The Zoo Story,* so goes the customary reading, Jerry confronts the vegetative Peter, forces him to stand his ground, dies finally on his own knife held in Peter's hand. In that suicidal act, Jerry becomes a scapegoat who gives his own life so that Peter will be knocked out of his complacency and learn to live, or LIVE. Even Albee believes this, or he said he did in answer to a question from Arthur Gelb (*The New York Times*, February 15, 1960): "Though he dies, he passes on an awareness of life to the other character in the play." If this is true, then presumably we are to take seriously—not as a dramatic device, but for its content—Jerry's "you have to make a start somewhere" speech in which he expounds the steps-to-love doctrine, a soggy inheritance from Carson McCullers ("A Tree. A Rock. A Cloud.") and Truman Capote (*The Grass Harp*). That the start should be something a great deal less gentle than the McCullers-Capote inheritance might suggest is not surprising when we consider that violence and death became twisted life symbols during the 1950's (as all the kids said after James Dean's fatal smashup, "Boy, that's living") and, then, turned literary in the 1960's (as in Jack Richardson's *Gallows Humor* and all the motorcycle movies from *The Wild Angels* to *Scorpio Rising*).

The problem with that reading is not that it is awash with adolescent profundity, which might well annoy some of the audience, but that it seems to be working against much that is going on within the play. Although Albee prepares the audience for the killing, it has always seemed gratuitous, a melodramatic flourish. The reason may be that it tries to suggest one thing (salvation) while the logic of the play demands something else. Except for a couple of expositional lapses, Jerry is too well drawn a character—self-pitying and aggressive, self-deluding and forlorn—to become the conventional "hero" (Albee uses that word in the Gelb interview) that the positive ending demands. He may well be so aware of his separation from everyone else that he plans or improvises ("could I have planned all this? No . . . no, I couldn't have. But I think I did") his own murder in a last desperate attempt to make contact, but there is nothing in the play to indicate that he succeeds. At the end, Peter is plainly a man knocked off his balance, but there is no indication that he has fallen into "an awareness of life." In fact, the play we are watching has already been presented in miniature in the dog story, and all Jerry gained from that encounter was "solitary but free passage." "There are some things in it that I don't really understand," Albee told Gelb. One of them may be that the play itself denies the romantic ending.

Virginia Woolf is a more slippery case. Here, too, the play works against the presumably upbeat ending, but Albee may be more aware that this is happening. According to the conventions of Broadway psychology, as reflected, for instance, in a play like William Inge's *The Dark at the Top of the Stairs,* in a moment of crisis two characters come to see themselves clearly. Out of their knowledge a new maturity is born, creating an intimacy that has not existed before and a community that allows them to face their problems (if not solve them) with new courage. This was the prevailing cliché of the serious Broadway play of the 1950's, and it was still viable enough in the 1960's to take over the last act of Lorraine Hansberry's *The Sign in Sidney Brustein's Window* and turn an interesting play into a conventional one. *Virginia Woolf* uses, or is used by, this cliché.

Although the central device of the play is the quarrel between George and Martha, the plot concerns their nonexistent son. From George's "Just don't start on the bit, that's all," before Nick and Honey enter, the play builds through hints, warnings, revelations until "sonny-Jim" [5] is created and then destroyed. Snap, goes the illusion. Out of the ruins, presumably, new strength comes. The last section, which is to be played "very softly, very slowly," finds George offering new tenderness to Martha, assuring her that the time had come for the fantasy to die, forcing her—no longer maliciously—to admit that she is afraid of Virginia Woolf. It is "Time for bed," and there is nothing left for them to do but go together to face the dark at the top of the stairs. As though the rejuvenation were not clear enough from the last scene, there is the confirming testimony in Honey's tearful reiteration "I want a child" and Nick's broken attempt to sympathize, "I'd like to. . . ." Then, too, the last act is called "The Exorcism," a name that had been the working title for the play itself.

As neat as Inge, and yet there is something wrong with it. How can a relationship like that of Martha and George, built so consistently on illusion (the playing of games), be expected to have gained something from a sudden admission of truth? What confirmation is there in Nick and Honey when we remember that she is drunk and hysterical and that he is regularly embarrassed by what he is forced to watch? There are two possibilities beyond the conventional reading suggested

[5] One of the "echoes"—to use Albee's word (*The Best Plays of 1964–1965*) for the unanchored allusions in *Tiny Alice*—must surely be a song that little boys used to sing: "Lulu had a baby,/Named it Sonny Jim,/Threw it in the piss-pot/To see if it could swim."

above. The last scene between Martha and George may be another one of their games; the death of the child may not be the end of illusion but an indication that the players have to go back to GO and start again their painful trip to home. Although there are many indications that George and Martha live a circular existence, going over the same ground again and again, the development of the plot and the tone of the last scene (the use of monosyllables, for instance, instead of their customary rhetoric) seem to deny that the game is still going on. The other possibility is that the truth—as in *The Iceman Cometh*—brings not freedom but death. To believe otherwise is to accept the truth-maturity cliché as readily as one must buy the violence-life analogy to get the positive ending of *The Zoo Story*. My own suspicion is that everything that feels wrong about the end of *Virginia Woolf* arises from the fact that, like the stabbing in *Zoo*, it is a balance-tipping ending that conventional theater says is positive but the Albee material insists is negative. . . .

The Theatre of the Absurd:
Edward Albee

by Martin Esslin

. . . Edward Albee (born in 1928) comes into the category of the Theatre of the Absurd precisely because his work attacks the very foundations of American optimism. His first play, *The Zoo Story* (1958), which shared the bill at the Provincetown Playhouse with Beckett's *Krapp's Last Tape,* already showed the forcefulness and bitter irony of his approach. In the realism of its dialogue and in its subject matter—an outsider's inability to establish genuine contact with a dog, let alone any human being—*The Zoo Story* is closely akin to the world of Harold Pinter. But the effect of this brilliant one-act duologue between Jerry, the outcast, and Peter, the conformist bourgeois, is marred by its melodramatic climax; when Jerry provokes Peter into drawing a knife and then impales himself on it, the plight of the schizophrenic outcast is turned into an act of sentimentality, especially as the victim expires in touching solicitude and fellow-feeling for his involuntary murderer.

But after an excursion into grimly realistic social criticism (the one-act play *The Death of Bessie Smith,* a re-creation of the end of the blues singer Bessie Smith in Memphis in 1937; she died after a motor accident because hospitals reserved for whites refused to admit her), Albee produced a play that clearly takes up the style and subject-matter of the Theatre of the Absurd and translates it into a genuine American idiom. *The American Dream* (1959–60; first performed at the York Playhouse, New York, on 24 January 1961) fairly and squarely attacks the ideals of progress, optimism, and faith in the national mission, and pours scorn on the sentimental ideals of family life, togetherness, and physical fitness; the euphemistic language and unwillingness to face the ultimate facts of the human condition that in America, even more than in Europe, represent the essence of bourgeois assumptions and attitudes. *The American Dream* shows an American family—Mommy, Daddy, Grandma—in search of a replacement for the adopted child that went wrong and died. The missing member of the family arrives in the shape of a gorgeous young man, the embodiment of the American dream, who admits that he consists only of muscles and a healthy exterior, but is dead inside, drained of genuine feeling and the capacity for experience. He will do anything for money—so he will even consent to become a member of the family. The language of *The American Dream* resembles that of Ionesco in its masterly combination of clichés. But these clichés, in their euphemistic, baby-talk tone, are as characteristically American as Ionesco's are French. The most disagreeable verities are hidden behind the corn-fed cheeriness of advertising jingles and family-magazine unctuousness. There are very revealing contrasts in the way these writers of different nationalities use the clichés of their own countries—the mechanical hardness of Ionesco's French platitudes; the flat, repetitive obtuseness of Pinter's English nonsense dialogue; and the oily glibness and sentimentality of the American cliché in Albee's promising and brilliant first example of an American contribution to the Theatre of the Absurd.

With his first full-length play *Who's Afraid of Virginia Woolf?* (first performed in New York on 14 October 1962) Albee achieved his breakthrough into the first rank of contemporary American playwrights. On the surface this is a savage marital battle in the tradition of Strindberg and the later O'Neill. George, the unsuccessful academic, his ambitious wife, and the young couple they are entertaining, are realistic characters; their world, that of drink-sodden and frustrated university teachers, is wholly real. But a closer inspection reveals elements which clearly still relate the play to Albee's earlier work and the Theatre of the Absurd. George and Martha (there are echoes there of George and Martha Washington) have an imaginary child which they treat as real, until in the cold dawn of that wild night they decide to 'kill' it by abandoning their joint fantasy. Here the connexion to *The American Dream* with its horrid dream-child of the ideal all-American boy becomes clear; thus there are elements of dream and allegory in the play (is the dream-child which cannot become real among people torn by ambition and lust something like the American ideal itself?); and there is also a Genet-like ritualistic element in its structure as a sequence of three rites: act I—'Fun and Games'; act II—'*Walpurgis-nacht*'; act III—'Exorcism'.

With *Tiny Alice* (1963) Albee broke new ground in a play which clearly tried to evolve a complex image of man's search for truth and certainty in a constantly shifting world, without ever wanting to construct a complete allegory or to offer any solutions to the questions he raised. Hence the indignant reaction of some critics seems to have been based on a profound misunderstanding. The play shows its hero buffeted between the church and the world of cynical wisdom and forced by the church to abandon his vocation for the priesthood to marry a rich woman who made a vast donation dependent on his decision. Yet immediately the marriage is concluded the lady and her staff depart, leaving the hero to a lonely death. The central image of the play is the mysterious model of the great mansion in which the action takes place, that occupies the centre of the stage. Inside this model every room corresponds to one in the real house, and tiny figures can be observed repeating the movements of the people who occupy it.* Everything that happens in the macrocosm is exactly repeated in the microcosm of the model. And no doubt inside the model there is another smaller model, which duplicates everything that happens on an even tinier scale, and so on *ad infinitum*, upwards and downwards on the scale of being. It is futile to search for the philosophical meaning of such an image. What it communicates is a mood, a sense of the mystery, the impenetrable complexity of the universe. And that is precisely what a dramatic poet is after.

With *A Delicate Balance* (1966) Albee returned to a more realistic setting which, however, is also deeply redolent of mystery and nameless fears, while *Box* and *Quotations from Mao Tse-Tung* (1968) returns to an openly absurdist convention by constructing an intricate pattern of cross-cut monologues, some emerging from tangible people (chairman Mao, a talkative lady), one from an empty box.

* [In fact no such figures are mentioned in the play although the butler does speculate as to the effect of such a discovery.—Ed.]

/

Albee and the Absurd: *The American Dream* and *The Zoo Story*

by Brian Way

As the American dramatist is often torn between a desire for the apparent security of realism and the temptation to experiment, so in Edward Albee's work, we see a tension between realism and the theatre of the absurd. *The Death of Bessie Smith* is a purely realistic play, and *Who's Afraid of Virginia Woolf?* is, for all its showiness, no more than a cross between sick drawing-room comedy and naturalistic tragedy. *The Zoo Story, The Sandbox* and *The American Dream* are, on the face of it, absurd plays, and yet, if one compares them with the work of Beckett, Ionesco or Pinter, they all retreat from the full implications of the absurd when a certain point is reached. Albee still believes in the validity of reason—that things can be proved, or that events can be shown to have definite meanings—and, unlike Beckett and the others, is scarcely touched by the sense of living in an absurd universe. Interesting and important as his plays are, his compromise seems ultimately a failure of nerve—a concession to those complementary impulses towards cruelty and self-pity which are never far below the surface of his work.

Albee has been attracted to the theatre of the absurd mainly, I think, because of the kind of social criticism he is engaged in. Both *The Zoo Story* and *The American Dream* are savage attacks on the American Way of Life. (I put the phrase in capitals to emphasize that this is not necessarily the way people in America actually live—simply that it is a pattern to which many Americans tend to conform, and, above all, that in the comics, on television, in advertising, and whenever an agency projects the personality of a politician, this is the way in which Ameri-

"Albee and the Absurd: *The American Dream* and *The Zoo Story*" by Brian Way. From John Russell Brown and Bernard Harris, eds., *American Theatre* (London: Edward Arnold [Publishers] Limited, 1967). Copyright © 1967 by Edward Arnold (Publishers) Limited. Reprinted by permission of the publisher.

cans are assumed and expected to live.) Earlier satirists, like Sinclair Lewis and H. L. Mencken, had made their attack through a heightened, but basically realistic, picture of representative men and social habits —Babbitt and the business-world, Elmer Gantry and religion—but this method is no longer appropriate. The American Way of Life has become a political slogan and a commercial vested interest since the war, and is maintained and manipulated through a conscious process of image-building carried out mainly by the mass-media of communication. A would-be social critic of today has to concern himself with these images rather than with representative men, and for the deflation of images realism is not necessarily the most effective artistic convention.

The American Way of Life, in the sense in which I am using the phrase, is a structure of images; and the images, through commercial and political exploitation, have lost much of their meaning. When the Eisenhower family at prayer becomes a televised political stunt, or the family meal an opportunity for advertising frozen foods, the image of the family is shockingly devalued. The deception practised is more complex than a simple lie: it involves a denial of our normal assumptions about evidence—about the relation between the observed world and its inner reality. This is why the techniques of the theatre of the absurd, which is itself preoccupied with the devaluation of language and of images, and with the deceptive nature of appearances, are so ideally suited to the kind of social criticism Albee intends. It is for this reason, too, that he has felt able to use the techniques of the theatre of the absurd, while stopping short of an acceptance of the metaphysic of the absurd upon which the techniques are based. It is possible, clearly, to see the absurd character of certain social situations without believing that the whole of life is absurd. In Albee's case, however, this has meant a restriction of scope, and his plays do not have the poetic quality or imaginative range of *Waiting for Godot,* for instance, or *The Caretaker,* or *Rhinoceros.*

The absurd, then, in so far as it interests the student of literature, presents itself for discussion on two levels: first, there is an underlying vision of the universe, a vision memorably expressed by Kafka and the existentialists as well as by the dramatists of the absurd; and secondly, a number of forms of writing and strategies of presentation generated by the underlying vision.

A writer's vision is absurd when the arbitrary, the disconnected, the irrelevant, non-reason, are seen to be the main principle or non-prin-

ciple of the universe. Pascal, whom existentialists sometimes claim as a
precursor, has expressed the vision most succinctly when he writes:

> Je m'effraie et m'étonne de me voir ici plutôt que là, car il n'y a
> point de raison pourquoi ici plutôt que là, pourquoi à présent plutôt
> que lor.[1]

Jean-Paul Sartre has the most complete and celebrated account of the
experience in *La Nausée*, where Roquentin sits on a park bench and
stares at the root of a chestnut tree. When, later, he tries to characterize
the experience, the word Absurdity comes to him:

> Un geste, un événement dans le petit monde calorié des hommes
> n'est jamais absurde que relativement: par rapport aux circonstances
> qui l'accompagnent. Les discours d'un fou, par exemple, sont absurdes
> par rapport à la situation où il se trouve mais non par rapport à son
> délire. Mais moi, tout à l'heure, j'ai fait l'expérience de l'absolu: l'absolu
> ou l'absurde. Cette racine, il n'y avait rien par rapport à quoi elle ne
> fût absurde . . . Absurde: par rapport aux cailloux, aux touffes d'herbe
> jaune, à la boue sèche, à l'arbre, au ciel, aux bancs verts. Absurde
> irréductible; rien—pas même un délire profond et secret de la nature
> —ne pouvait l'expliquer. Évidemment je ne savais pas tout, je n'avais
> pas vu le germe se développer ni l'arbre croître. Mais devant cette grosse
> patte rugueuse, ni l'ignorance ni le savoir n'avait d'importance: le
> monde des explications et des raisons n'est pas celui de l'existence.
> J'avais beau répéter: 'C'est une racine'—ça ne prenait plus. Je voyais
> bien qu'on ne pouvait pas passer de sa fonction de racine, de pompe
> aspirante, *à ça*, à cette peau dure et compacte de phoque, à cet aspect
> huileux, calleux, entêté. La fonction n'expliquait rien: elle permettait
> de comprendre en gros ce que c'était qu'une racine, mais pas du tout
> *celle-eci*.[2]

---

[1] "I am frightened and amazed to see myself here rather than there, since there
is no reason at all why 'here' rather than 'there,' why 'now' rather than 'then.'"
Quoted by P. Foulquié, *L'Existentialisme* (Paris, 1952), p. 39.

[2] "A gesture, an event, in the cosy little world of men is never absurd except
relatively: in relation to the circumstances which accompany it. The words of a
madman, for example, are only absurd in relation to the situation he is in, but
not in relation to his delirium. But I, just now, experienced the absolute: the
absolute or the absurd. There was nothing in relation to which this root was not
absurd . . . Absurd: in relation to the pebbles, the tufts of yellow grass, the dry
mud, the tree, the sky, the green benches. Absurd, irreducible: nothing—not even
a profound secret delirium of nature—could explain it. Obviously I did not know
everything, I had not seen the seed develop, nor the tree grow. But in front of this
great gnarled foot, neither ignorance nor knowledge had any importance: the
world of explanations and reasons is not that of existence . . . It was useless for

Both Pascal and Sartre describe vividly the arbitrary, dislocated quality of experience—the sense of living in a world where nothing has any fundamental connection with anything else. Sartre goes a stage further when he exposes the irrelevance and the futility of reason—the reason in which the naturalist writer has supreme faith—and the completely illusory nature of rational explorations. When one says to oneself "It's a root" and continues in a generalizing abstracting way to explain to oneself what it is that a root does in relation to the tree and the earth, one is deceiving oneself if one imagines that the process brings one any nearer to understanding *that*—that object which is unique, stubborn (entêté), and, as Roquentin says a little later, "beneath any possible explanation" ("au-dessous de toute explication"). There is no transition from the world of explanations to the world of the absurd; from the notion that a root is a suction pump to the thing itself—the bark tough and close as a seal's skin, the greasy stubborn horny thing before Roquentin's eyes.

A writer for whom experiences are as dislocated and unrelated as this must clearly deny the logic of cause and effect, the logic on which naturalistic drama is based. Sartre expresses this denial in a particularly interesting way in the sequence of reflections from which I have already quoted:

> Des arbres, des piliers bleu de nuit, le râle heureux d'une fontaine, des odeurs vivantes, des petits brouillards de chaleur qui flottait dans l'air froid, un homme roux qui digérait sur un banc: toutes ces somnolences, toutes *ces* digestions prises ensemble offraient un aspect vaguement comique. Comique . . . non: ça n'allait pas jusque-là, rien de ce qui existe ne peut être comique; c'était comme une analogie flottante, presque insaisissable avec certaines situations de vaudeville.[3]

"Comique . . . non . . . une analogie flottante . . . avec certaines situations de vaudeville"—incidents, that is, which have the logic of music-hall slapstick, but which are not necessarily funny. In music-hall

---

me to repeat: "It is a root"—that didn't fit any longer. I saw very well that one could not move from its function as a root, as a suction pump, *to that,* to that tough close seal's skin, to that greasy, horny, stubborn appearance. Its function explained nothing: it allowed one to understand in a general way what a root was, but not at all what *this* was" (*La Nausée* (Paris, 1942), pp. 168–9).

[3] "Trees, midnight blue pillars, the happy chatter of a fountain, vivid scents, light warm vapours floating in the cold air, a red-haired man digesting his lunch on a bench: all this drowsing and digestion taken as a whole had a vaguely comic aspect. Comic . . . no, it didn't go quite as far as that, nothing which exists can be comic; it was like a fleeting analogy, almost impossible to grasp, with certain music-hall situations" (*La Nausée* (Paris, 1942), p. 167).

acts and in the slapstick situations of the early cinema we see constantly this denial of the logic of cause and effect on which Sartre's
analogy is based: in *City Lights* a statue is being unveiled; we expect a
dignified climax to a public ceremony, but instead we find Chaplin
cradled in the statue's arms making frantic efforts to climb down.
Similarly in Ionesco's *Rhinoceros,* in which the citizens of a French
provincial town are being rapidly transformed into rhinoceroses, the
telephone rings, and Bérenger picks it up, with certain reasonable expectations as to whom his correspondent will be:

> *Bérenger.* Perhaps the authorities have decided to take action at last; maybe
> they're ringing to ask our help in whatever measures they've decided to
> adopt.
> *Daisy.* I'd be surprised if it was them.
> [*The telephone rings again.*]
> *Bérenger.* It is the authorities, I tell you, I recognize the ring—a long-
> drawn-out ring, I can't ignore an appeal from them. It can't be anyone
> else. [*He picks up the receiver.*] Hallo? [*Trumpetings are heard com-
> ing from the receiver.*] You hear that? Trumpeting! Listen!
> [*Daisy puts the telephone to her ear, is shocked by the sound, quickly re-
> places the receiver.*]
> *Daisy* [*frightened*]. What's going on?
> *Bérenger.* They're playing jokes now.
> *Daisy.* Jokes in bad taste!

(p. 99)

Bérenger, an inveterate believer in the logic of cause and effect, a man
who is certain he lives in a meaningful universe, picks up the telephone
and instead of the reassuring voice of the authorities hears the trumpet-
ing of rhinoceroses. It is indeed, as Daisy says, a joke in bad taste—
"Comique . . . non . . . une analogie flottante . . . avec certaines
situations de vaudeville." There could be no more vivid dramatic instance of what it means to live in an absurd universe.

The absurdist habit of mind, then, is overwhelmingly intellectualist,
metaphysical even. It constantly asks the question "What is the meaning of life?," and finds as an answer, "There is no meaning," or, "We
do not know," a discovery which may be horrifying or comic, or both.
The theatre of the absurd has responded to this metaphysic by evolving
new dramatic forms,[4] and the second stage of my analysis of the absurd
will be an examination of these.

[4] Perhaps it would be more accurate to say that it is an attempt to bring together a number of old theatrical devices in a new way; see "The Tradition of the
Absurd" in Esslin, pp. 233–89.

For the playwright who accepts without reservations that he is living in an absurd universe, the loss of faith in reason which is at the heart of this vision and the conviction that the rational exploration of experience is a form of self-deception, imply a rejection of those theatrical conventions which reflect a belief in reason. Characters with fixed identities; events which have a definite meaning; plots which assume the validity of cause and effect; dénouements which offer themselves as complete resolutions of the questions raised by the play; and language which claims to mean what it says—none of these can be said to be appropriate means for expressing the dislocated nature of experience in an absurd world. In terms of formal experiment, then, the theatre of the absurd represents a search for images of non-reason.

Albee has used these images of non-reason in his attack on the American Way of Life without, as I have said, accepting the underlying vision which generated them. His work belongs to the second level of the theatre of the absurd: it shows a brilliantly inventive sense of what can be done with the techniques, but stops short of the metaphysic which makes the techniques completely meaningful. Nevertheless, *The American Dream* and *The Zoo Story* are the most exciting productions of the American theatre in the last fifteen years, and I propose to analyse them in detail in such a way as to bring out particularly what they have in common with other absurd plays and where they diverge from them.

In *The American Dream* (1961), Albee is closer to Ionesco than to any other dramatist. Like Ionesco, he sees the absurd localized most sharply in conventions of social behaviour. For both dramatists, the normal currency of social intercouse—of hospitality, or courtesy, or desultory chat—has lost its meaning, and this "devaluation of language," to use Martin Esslin's invaluable phrase, is an index for them of the vacuity of the social life represented. The inane civilities exchanged by the Smiths and the Martins in *The Bald Prima Donna* enact the complete absence of human contact which is the reality beneath the appearance of communication. We see similar effects in *The American Dream* in the opening exchanges:

> *Daddy.* Uh . . . Mrs. Barker, is it? Won't you sit down?
> *Mrs. Barker.* I don't mind if I do.
> *Mommy.* Would you like a cigarette, and a drink, and would you like to cross your legs?

Mrs. Barker. You forget yourself, Mommy; I'm a professional woman. But
  I will cross my legs.
Daddy. Yes, make yourself comfortable.
Mrs. Baker. I don't mind if I do.*   (p. 28)

Ionesco and Albee use this method of exposing the essential meaninglessness of most middle-class language and gesture as a basis for much
wider effects than the mere deflation of certain speech-habits. In
Ionesco, particularly, it becomes a major principle of dramatic construction. He subjects conventional patterns of behaviour, the clichés
of which much everyday speech is entirely composed, and the most
complacent and unthinking of our normal assumptions and attitudes,
to a disturbing shift of perspective: he places them in grotesque situations where they are ludicrously inappropriate, and their meaninglessness is stripped bare. *Amédée* (1954) is probably his most elaborate
exercise in this technique. Amédée and Madeleine Buccinioni, a
middle-aged bourgeois couple, have shut themselves up in their Paris
apartment for fifteen years in order to conceal the corpse of a man
Amédée may have murdered. The corpse has grown a white beard and
long fingernails and toenails over the years, but during Act I, its rate of
growth is suddenly accelerated, presenting Amédée and Madeleine with
an acute problem:

Madeleine. The neighbours must have heard.
Amédée [stopping]. They *may* not have done. *[Short silence.]* There's not
  a sound from them! . . . Besides, at this time of day . . .
Madeleine. They must have heard something. They're not all deaf . . .
Amédée. Not *all* of them, they couldn't be. But as I say, at this time of
  day . . .
Madeleine. What could we tell them?
Amédée. We could say it was the postman!
*Madeleine [turning her back to the audience and looking towards the
  rear window].* It was the postman who did it! It was the p-o-stman!
  [To Amédée]. Will they believe us? The postman must have gone, by
  now.
Amédée. All the better. *[Loudly shouting to the rear of the stage.]* It was
  the p-o–stman!
Madeleine.⎫
Amédée.   ⎬ It was the p-o–stman! The p-o–stman!
[They stop shouting, and the echo is heard.]

* References to *The American Dream* and *The Zoo Story* are from *The Zoo Story
and Other Plays* (London, 1962).

Echo. The p–o–stman! The p–o–stman! P–o–stman! O–o–stman!

Amédée [*he and Madeleine both turning to face the audience*]. You see, even the echo is repeating it.

Madeleine. Perhaps it isn't the echo!

Amédée. It strengthens our case, anyhow. It's an alibi! . . . Let's sit down.

Madeleine [*sitting down*]. Life's really getting impossible. Where are we to find new window-panes?

[*Suddenly, from the adjoining room, a violent bang is heard against the wall; Amédée, who was about to sit down, stands up again, his gaze rivetted on the left of the stage; Madeleine does the same.*]

Madeleine [*uttering a cry*]. Ah!

Amédée [*distractedly*]. Keep calm, keep calm!

[*The left-hand door gradually gives way, as though under steady pressure.*]

Madeleine [*not far from fainting, but still standing, cries out again*]. Ah, Heaven help us!

[*Then Amédée and Madeleine, dumb with terror, watch two enormous feet slide slowly in through the open door and advance about eighteen inches on to the stage.*]

Madeleine. Look!

[*This is naturally an anguished cry, yet there should be a certain restraint about it; it should, of course, convey fear, but above all, irritation. This is an embarrassing situation, but it should not seem at all unusual, and the actors should play this scene quite naturally. It is a 'nasty blow' of course, an extremely 'nasty blow,' but no worse than that.*]   (pp. 176–8)

The dialogue is composed entirely of clichés, and is dominated by mundane bourgeois attitudes—chiefly the anxiety to preserve appearances before neighbours, and the desperate determination to act as if everything were normal. (Ionesco's final stage direction, of course, underlines this.) As so often in absurd drama, the language and the action contradict each other. The grotesque horror of the situation is played off against the ludicrous pretence at maintaining a sense of the ordinary suggested by the language. When middle-class clichés and stock attitudes are shown to be so evidently meaningless in this situation, one is directed to the conclusion that they are in fact meaningless in all situations, and that only the blindness of habit conceals this fact from us.

Albee develops the situation in *The American Dream* along similar lines. He sees the American Way of Life as one in which normal human feelings and relationships have been deprived of meaning. The gestures of love, sexual attraction, parental affection, family feeling and hospitality remain, but the actual feelings which would give the gestures meaning have gone. To show this in sharp dramatic terms, Albee constructs a situation of gestures which are normally supposed to have meaning but, as transposed by him, are seen to have none. As soon as the family tableau of Mommy and Daddy, the overtly homey middle-aged couple, and Grandma, their apparent tribute to the duty of caring for the aged, is presented, we see what Albee is doing:

Mommy. We were very poor! But then I married you, Daddy, and now we're very rich.
Daddy. Grandma isn't rich.
Mommy. No, but you've been so good to Grandma she feels rich. She doesn't know you'd like to put her in a nursing home.
Daddy. I wouldn't!
Mommy. Well, heaven knows *I* would! I can't stand it, watching her do the cooking and the housework, polishing the silver, moving the furniture. . . .
Daddy. She likes to do that. She says it's the least she can do to earn her keep.
Mommy. Well, she's right. You can't live off people . . . I have a right to live off you because I married you, and because I used to let you get on top of me and bump your uglies; and I have a right to all your money when you die. And when you do, Grandma and I can live by ourselves . . . if she's still here. Unless you have her put away in a nursing home.
Daddy. I have no intention of putting her in a nursing home.
Mommy. Well, I wish somebody would do something with her!
Daddy. At any rate you're very well provided for.
Mommy. You're my sweet Daddy; that's very nice.
Daddy. I love my Mommy.   (pp. 21–2)

The characters are isolated from each other in little worlds of selfishness, impotence and lovelessness, and all warmth of human contact is lost. It would be inaccurate to say that the gestures of love and connection ("You're my sweet Daddy"—"I love my Mommy") are deflated; their meaninglessness is exposed by tagging them on as afterthoughts to phases of the action where they are—as here—ludicrously inapplicable.

This method of scene-construction determines not only the local effects of *The American Dream,* but the major patterns of the play. Albee is disturbed and agonized by the extent of the dislocation of people's relationships and the imprisoning isolation of which these scenes are images. The play's central image of this failure of human feeling and contact is sterility—the inability to beget or bear a child—

and as its title suggests, Albee tries to give the image the widest possible social reference. He implies that the sterility which the audience sees in his characters is typical of the society as a whole, and is created and perpetuated by the society. For him, the American Way of Life systematically eliminates, in the name of parental care, and social and moral concern, every trace of natural human feeling and every potentiality for warm human contact from those who have to live by it, and especially from the young.

When Mommy, Daddy and Grandma, and the quality of their lives, have been firmly established, Mrs. Barker, a representative of the Bye-Bye Adoption Service, calls on them. She forgets why she has called (a common motif in absurd plays, underlying the arbitrariness and irrelevance of all action in an absurd world, though little more than a gimmick here). Grandma, to help her, gives her a "hint"—the story of "a man very much like Daddy, and a woman very much like Mommy," and "a dear lady" very much like Mrs. Barker. It is a story of individual sterility:

> The woman who was very much like Mommy, said that she and the man who was very much like Daddy had never been blessed with anything very much like a bumble of joy . . .
> . . . she said that they wanted a bumble of their own, but that the man, who was very much like Daddy, couldn't have a bumble; and the man, who was very much like Daddy, said that yes, they had wanted a bumble of their own, but that the woman, who was very much like Mommy, couldn't have one and that now they wanted to buy something very much like a bumble.   (p. 40)

It is also a story of that collective sterility which eliminates natural impulses in others. Mommy and Daddy buy "a bumble of joy," and its upbringing is a series of mutilations at their hands:

> *Grandma.* . . . *then,* it began to develop an interest in its you-know-what.
> *Mrs. Barker.* In its you-know-what! Well! I hope they cut its hands off at the wrists!
> *Grandma.* Well, yes, they did that eventually. But first, they cut off its you-know-what.
> *Mrs. Barker.* A much better idea!
> *Grandma.* That's what they thought. But after they cut off its you-know-what, it *still* put its hands under the covers, *looking* for its you-know-what. So, finally, they had to cut off its hands at the wrists.   (pp. 40–1)

The child's eyes are gouged out, it is castrated, its hands are cut off, its tongue is cut out, and finally it dies. In this brilliant sequence of dramatic writing, Albee has given us a fable of his society, where all the capabilities for connection—eyes to see, sexual organs with which to love, hands to touch, and tongue to speak—are destroyed, and the victim of the socializing process of the American Way of Life, humanly speaking, dies. And it is all done in the name of affection and care. Once again, the gestures of human contact survive grotesquely in the coyness with which the sexual act and the begetting and rearing of children are described ("being blessed with a bumble of joy," "its you-know-what"), and the gestures are seen to be hideously and mockingly at odds with the reality.

Towards the end of the play, the victim himself appears—the "twin" of "the bumble of joy." He is a young man with all the external marks of youth and vitality, handsome, muscular and self-confident. Grandma recognizes in him immediately the American Dream. But just as the gestures of parental love have been only a sham, his outwardly vigorous youthful appearance is only a shell. His life is a terrible emptiness, a series of deprivations identical with the mutilations practised on his "twin" brother:

> I don't know what became of my brother . . . to the rest of myself . . . except that, from time to time, in the years that have passed, I have suffered losses . . . that I can't explain. A fall from grace . . . a departure of innocence . . . loss . . . loss. . . . Once . . . it was as if all at once my heart . . . became numb . . . almost as though I . . . almost as though . . . just like that . . . it had been wrenched from my body . . . and from that time I have been unable to love . . .
>
> And there is more . . . there are more losses, but it all comes down to this: I no longer have the capacity to feel anything. I have no emotions. I have been drained, torn asunder . . . disembowelled. I have, now, only my person . . . my body, my face. I use what I have . . . I let people love me . . . I accept the syntax around me, for while I cannot relate . . . I know I must be related *to* . . .   (pp. 50–1)

This moving speech is one of those moments of total illumination in absurd drama (Aston's account of his experiences in the psychiatric ward in *The Caretaker* is the finest example) where a character, for a moment, sees the entire hopelessness and confusion of his existence before lapsing once more into the "syntax around" him. The Young Man has to accept that syntax—the meaningless gestures of human affection and contact—when he is adopted, or re-adopted, by Mommy and Daddy. While they celebrate with Sauterne, Grandma observes sardonically from the wings: "Well, I guess that just about wraps it up. I mean, for better or worse, this is a comedy . . ." The bad Sauterne is drunk, and sterility, impotence, lovelessness and disconnection are masked with the gestures of celebration, conviviality and family-love, suggesting as they do all that is lacking—the physical warmth of sex and parenthood, and the meaningfulness of people being together. Only the gestures remain, these gestures which have been simultaneously canonized and deprived of meaning by the publicists of the American Way of Life: the politicians, the admen, the columnists and the TV commentators.

It is significant that the only character in *The American Dream* with any vitality or attractiveness is Grandma—and she is "rural," from an older way of life. The way in which she is juxtaposed against the Young Man who is the American Dream seems to symbolize a society in which the natural order of life has been reversed, in which the younger one is the less chance one has of being alive.

These patterns and images occur elsewhere in Albee's work. His sense of human isolation and despair is the central preoccupation of *The Death of Bessie Smith* (a bad play, it seems to me), and in *The Sandbox,* which parallels the situation of *The American Dream* most interestingly, though on too cramped a stage. The image of sterility is very prominent in *Who's Afraid of Virginia Woolf?,* but is used there much less effectively than in *The American Dream.* Apart from its spectacular ability to amuse and shock, *Virginia Woolf* has a certain emptiness—no incident or image in it has reference to anything wider than the neuroses of its characters.

His first play, *The Zoo Story* (1959), however, contains some very fine dramatic writing. Again it is an exploration of the farce and the agony of human isolation. When the play opens, Peter, a prosperous youngish man in the publishing business, is reading on a bench in Central Park, New York. Jerry, who describes himself as a "permanent transient," insists on talking to Peter. Peter tries to brush him off, to get on with his reading, but Jerry forces Peter to confront him fully as a human being, working first on his curiosity, and then provoking him by insults and blows. When Peter is sufficiently enraged, they fight. Jerry, in an improbable and sentimental catastrophe, puts a knife in Peter's hand and impales himself on it. He succeeds in forcing Peter out from behind the shelter of his possessions (symbolized by the park bench over which they ostensibly fight) and his middle-class complacency, into a real confrontation with the isolation and despair of the human condition. If Jerry is a "permanent transient," Peter is, after the killing, at least "dispossessed":

> You won't be coming back here any more, Peter; you've been dispossessed. You've lost your bench, but you've defended your honor.
>
> (p. 142)

And Jerry, in turn, even if it has cost him his life, has at last made "contact" with another being.

It is because human isolation is so great, and because the "contact" which would end it is so formidably difficult to obtain, that Jerry went to the zoo:

> Now I'll let you in on what happened at the zoo; but first, I should tell you why I went to the zoo. I went to the zoo to find out more about the way people exist with animals, and the way animals exist with each other, and with people too. It probably wasn't a fair test, what with everyone separated by bars from everyone else, the animals for the most part from each other, and always the people from the animals. But if it's a zoo, that's the way it is. (p. 135)

The entire human condition, for Jerry, is a zoo story of people (and animals) forever separated by bars.

In its finest scene, the long speech in which Jerry describes his attempt to form a relationship with his landlady's dog, *The Zoo Story* offers a superb example of what I call pseudo-crisis—the second pattern of absurd writing that is central to Albee's work. In classic drama, crisis is one of the most important means by which the action is significantly advanced. In *Othello,* for instance, when Iago tells Othello that he has seen Desdemona's handkerchief in Cassio's hands, a whole complex of tensions is brought to a head, and after this crisis, the catastrophe is measurably nearer, and Othello is demonstrably a stage further on his course of violence and madness. In the absurd play, on the other hand, what I call a pseudo-crisis occurs when a similar complex of tensions is brought to a head without resolving anything, without contributing to any development or progression, serving in fact to demonstrate that nothing as meaningful as progression or development can occur, emphasizing that complexity and tension are permanent and unresolvable elements of a world of confusion. Lucky's speech in *Waiting for Godot* is perhaps the most elaborate and extreme occurrence. Harold Pinter's work, too, is full of pseudo-crisis, the funniest instance, perhaps, being Davies's account of his visit to the monastery at Luton in search of boots (*The Caretaker*).

Jerry's long speech in *The Zoo Story* has all the marks of pseudo-crisis. It is used here to explore Albee's preoccupation with man's failure to make contact with others, and the drying up of those feelings that should provide connection. Jerry lives in a rooming-house where the landlady's dog attacks him every time he comes in. He is fascinated by the dog's hatred; he responds to it with obsessive force: it is a challenge—the dog is intensely concerned about him and if he can meet the challenge he may be able to create out of it the contact he is looking for. He decides that first he will try to kill the dog with kindness, and if that fails he will simply kill it. He feeds it hamburgers; its animosity doesn't diminish, and so, at the climax of this pseudo-crisis— a farcical and yet poignant parody of the love-hate situation in romantic fiction—he gives the dog a poisoned hamburger. Nothing really happens, nothing is resolved. The dog doesn't die, nor does it come to love Jerry; for a moment Jerry and the dog look at each other, but then the dog withdraws from contact with him; even the pressure of its hatred has gone—"We neither love nor hurt because we do not try to reach each other," Jerry says, trying to express the agony of his need:

> I loved the dog now, and I wanted him to love me. I had tried to love and I had tried to kill, and both had been unsuccessful by themselves. . . . I hoped that the dog would understand.
>
> . . . it's just that if you can't deal with people, you have to make a start somewhere. WITH ANIMALS! (*much faster now, and like a conspirator*) . . . Don't you see? A person has to have some way of dealing with SOMETHING. If not with people . . . SOMETHING. With a bed, with a cockroach, with a mirror . . . no, that's too hard, that's one of the last steps. With a cockroach, with a . . . with a . . . with a carpet, with a roll of toilet paper . . . no, not that either . . . that's a mirror, too; always check bleeding. You see how hard it is to find things? With a street corner, and too many lights, all colours reflecting on the oily-wet streets . . . with a wisp of smoke, a wisp . . . of smoke . . . with . . . with . . . with love, with vomiting, with crying, with fury because the pretty little ladies, aren't pretty little ladies, with making money with your body which is an act of love and I could prove it, with howling because you're alive; with God. How about that? WITH GOD WHO IS A COLOURED QUEEN WHO WEARS A KIMONO AND PLUCKS HIS EYE-BROWS, WHO IS A WOMAN WHO CRIES WITH DETERMINATION BEHIND HER CLOSED DOOR . . . with God, who, I'm told, turned his back on the

whole thing some time ago . . . with . . . some day, with people . . .
(JERRY *sighs the next word heavily*) People. With an idea; a concept.
And where better, where ever better in this humiliating excuse for a jail,
where better to communicate one single, simple-minded idea than in an
entrance-hall? Where? It would be a START! Where better to make a
beginning . . . to understand and just possibly be understood . . .
than with . . . than with A DOG. Just that; a dog . . . A dog.

                                                              (pp. 130–2)

The dramatic structure of this part of Jerry's speech reflects very closely
the rhythms of pseudo-crisis—the excitement, the tensions, rising to
the shouted climax ("WITH GOD WHO IS . . ."), and then slipping away
into the lax despairing tempo of its inconclusive end ("with . . . some
day, with people"). The hopelessness of this is quickly recognized, and
Jerry reverts to his attempt with the dog, but this, too, has failed and
proved nothing. In this final downward curve of the pseudo-crisis
everything is conditional and hypothetical ("It would be A START!
Where better to make a beginning . . . to understand, and just possibly be understood . . .").

In this early play, there is an attempt, too, to relate Jerry's agony to
the wider social pattern—to see it as a product of the American Way
of Life:

> I am a *permanent transient,* and my home is in the sickening room-
> ing-houses on the West Side of New York City, which is the greatest
> city in the world. Amen.   (p. 133)

In spite of the bitter force of this, however, it is clear that the impulse
of social criticism has only been very partially translated into dramatic
terms. Jerry's outburst here tells the audience how to react; it is almost
a piece of editorializing, and doesn't have the persuasiveness of art, the
sense that ideas have become vision and are being enacted.

At such moments in *The Zoo Story,* and most of all, of course, at the
moment of Jerry's melodramatic and sentimental death, we are left
with a sense of dissatisfaction whose root causes are to be found in that
compromise with the experimental theatre that seems to me so characteristic of American dramatists. The action and the dialogue are dislocated, arbitrary and absurd (pre-eminently in Jerry's story of the dog)
up to the moment of Jerry's death, and then all the traditional assumptions of naturalism flood back into the play. It is postulated, quite as
firmly as in any Ibsen social drama, that a catastrophe is also a resolution of the situation of the play, and that events, however obscure,

ultimately have a definite and unambiguous meaning. Jerry spends his dying breath telling us what the play means as explicitly as does Lona Hessel at the end of *Pillars of Society.* This sudden reversion to a faith in the validity of rational explanations makes previous events in the play seem arbitrary in a wholly unjustifiable way: they can no longer be seen as appropriate symbols of life in an absurd universe. The slightest hint that events in an absurd play are amenable to everyday explanation is completely destructive of their dramatic effectiveness. If it were possible to say of Vladimir and Estragon, or of Davies, that they are crazy bums who should be locked up, *Waiting for Godot* and *The Caretaker* would be ruined. In spite of some striking effects, it is possible to entertain this suspicion about Jerry, and it is largely because of this misguided attempt to exploit the advantages both of the theatre of the absurd and of realism, that *The Zoo Story* misses the greatness which at times seems so nearly within its grasp.

The American Dream does not show so straightforward an evasion of the absurd as *The Zoo Story,* but it lacks even more completely the metaphysical dimension. One can perhaps best begin accounting for its limitations by noting a distinction which Martin Esslin makes most perceptively: first there is—

> . . . the experience that Ionesco expresses in plays like *The Bald Prima Donna* or *The Chairs,* Adamov in *La Parodie,* or N. F. Simpson in *A Resounding Tinkle.* It represents the satirical, paradistic aspect of the Theatre of the Absurd, its social criticism, its pillorying of an inauthentic, petty society. This may be the most easily accessible, and therefore most widely recognized, message of the Theatre of the Absurd, but it is far from being its most essential or most significant feature.
>
> Behind the satirical exposure of the absurdity of inauthentic ways of life, the Theatre of the Absurd is facing up to a deeper layer of absurdity—the absurdity of the human condition itself in a world where the decline of religious belief has deprived man of certainties.*
>
> (p. 292)

The American Dream is effective only within the limits of the first category. It is too exclusively and merely a satire of American middle-class aspirations and self-deceptions. It is, above all, a play about Other People, not about ourselves: when we laugh at Mommy and Daddy, we are laughing at emotional and sexual failures which we do not recognize as our own and in which we refuse to be implicated, whereas

---

* [Martin Esslin, *The Theatre of the Absurd* (New York, 1961).—Ed.]

when we laugh at Davies, or at Vladimir and Estragon, we are laughing
at our own illusions and recognizing our own acts of hubris, self-
deception and failure. Since *The American Dream* doesn't implicate
us, it never becomes tragic. Harold Pinter has said of his own play:

> As far as I am concerned *The Caretaker* is funny up to a point.
> Beyond that point it ceases to be funny, and it was because of that point
> that I wrote it.[5]

Albee never reached this point except perhaps for the brief moment I
have noted where the Young Man's sense of loss is met with Grandma's
compassion. But we do not otherwise have to regard the characters—
certainly not Mommy and Daddy—as tragic or even terrifying: they
enact for us a certain attitude to America in 1960; they do not go
beyond it to tell us anything about the human condition.

In one important sense, *The American Dream* does not belong even
to the "satirical, parodistic" category of absurd plays. It is, like *The Zoo
Story,* a play which reaches a definite conclusion and which implicitly
claims that its events have an unambiguous meaning. Grandma's "hint"
to Mrs. Barker is a fable of almost diagrammatic directness and simplicity; by contrast, the Fireman's fables in *The Bald Prima Donna* are
absurd parodies, satirizing the assumption that a tale has a "moral," and
further, undermining our confidence in the kind of popular wisdom
represented by the morals of Aesop's fables.

Above all, at the end of *The American Dream,* Grandma can tell the
audience:

> Well, I guess that just about wraps it up. I mean, for better or worse,
> this is a comedy, and I don't think we'd better go any further. No,
> definitely not. So let's leave things as they are right now . . . while
> everybody's happy . . . while everybody's got what he wants . . . or
> everybody's got what he thinks he wants. Good night, dears.

Her remark, "Well, I guess that just about wraps it up," is ironical only
in the most external sense—in the sense that Mommy and Daddy and
the Young Man and Mrs. Barker, who have all just drunk "To satisfaction," are in for some unpleasant surprises. As far as Grandma and
the audience are concerned the situation really is wrapped up, and the
play has proved its point as self-consciously as any theorem. Again,
The Bald Prima Donna is a significant contrast, ending not with a proof
but returning in a circle to the point at which it began.

---

[5] Letter to *Sunday Times* (14 August, 1960); quoted Esslin, p. 218.

It is only when one compares *The American Dream* with the greatest absurd plays that the real damage done by this compromise between reason and the absurd can be fully reckoned. In the first place, many of the local effects seem to be, in retrospect, merely tricks. The way in which it handles argument will illustrate what I mean. The metaphysic of the absurd, as I have said, involves a loss of faith in reason and in the validity of rational explorations of experience, and one of the most characteristic forms of writing of the absurd theatre, developed to represent this on the stage, is the systematic pursuit of the irrelevant. Absurd plays are full of arguments which lead nowhere, or which parody the processes of logic, or which are conducted from ludicrous premisses. At the beginning of *The American Dream* Mommy's account of her argument in the department store as to whether her hat was beige or wheat-colored is a clear instance of this. But it does not symbolize anything deeper: far from being an index of a world in which everything is too uncertain to be settled by argument, it takes its place in a play which, from its determination to prove a point, is naïvely confident in the power of argument. It therefore seems, in retrospect, no more than a trick to get the play started. By comparison, the argument in *Rhinoceros,* as to whether the animals which charged down the street had one horn or two, is funnier and also infinitely more disturbing: it represents the last feeble efforts of ordinary men to cling to their reassuring certitudes as their world founders into chaos, and, as they themselves, through turning into rhinoceroses, are about to lose their very identities. Albee's work lacks this imaginative dimension, to say nothing of the compassion, horror and despair, implicit in the periodic speculations of Vladimir and Estragon on the nature of Godot.

But it is in dénouements, as I have pointed out, that Albee diverges most clearly from the absurd, and it is here that the divergence does him most harm. His plays are tightly "wrapped up," where the best absurd plays leave us with an extended sense of the uncertainties of our condition. The quiet heartrending close of *Waiting for Godot—*

Vladimir. Well, shall we go?
Estragon. Yes, let's go.
They do not move.

—or the end of *The Caretaker,* where Davies and Aston look ahead into their bleak future, a future in which Davies will never "get settled down and fixed up," and in which Aston will never build his shed, have all the dramatic and poetic power Albee lacks. Perhaps the most relevant

comparison is with the lyrical closing moments of *Amédée*, where
Amédée, as he floats up into the sky, makes a speech to the crowd:

> Ladies and Gentlemen . . . Please don't think . . . I should like to
> stay . . . stay with my feet on the ground . . . It's against my will
> . . . I don't want to get carried away . . . I'm all for progress, I like
> to be of use to my fellow men . . . I believe in social realism . . .

As well as being delightfully comic, Amédée's flight into space even
while he utters all the positivist nostrums by which man tries to keep
his feet on the ground, is an exquisite poetic image, where Albee's
narrow cocksureness is poetically dead.

When all these limitations of scope have been noted, however, it is
only fair that one should return to an assertion of the importance of
Albee's good qualities in the American theatre. If it is true that he in-
habits a finite world, he does so with brilliance, inventiveness, intelligence and moral courage.

Symbolism and Naturalism in
Edward Albee's *The Zoo Story*

by Rose A. Zimbardo

The acclaim, both popular and critical, which has greeted Albee's
The Zoo Story leads one to speculate upon the direction American
drama is likely to take in the future. Concern with idea, rather than
character or plot, is not new in the American theatre, nor is the use
of symbolism for the realization of idea. There is, however, about
American plays which employ symbolism—from O'Neill to Williams
—a strong suggestion of the gimmick. Because American playwrights
have been self-conscious in employing symbols, their symbolism is almost always embarrassingly obvious. It calls attention to itself and exists
as a kind of scaffolding which the audience feels the playwright should
either have built over or removed. For example, O'Neill's symbolistic
drama, which has, of course, shaped all later American drama, directs
attention toward the symbol as symbol rather than upon a whole
dramatic structure within which symbolism operates. The audience
must identify the symbols and their equivalents to work out the play's
meaning. Symbol and meaning are, therefore, external to the play's
design. *Mourning Becomes Electra* provides an excellent example.

What marks *The Zoo Story* as a new development of our drama is
the way in which Albee blends symbolism with naturalism to realize
his theme. Somewhat startling is the realization that Albee's are traditional Christian symbols which, despite their modern dress, retain their
original significance—or, more precisely, express their original significance in modern terms. The relationship between traditional symbol and naturalistic dialogue, situation and setting is, however, never
forced, as it so often is in, say, a Williams' play. Rather symbolism is

"Symbolism and Naturalism in Edward Albee's *The Zoo Story*" by Rose A.
Zimbardo. From *Twentieth Century Literature*, VIII, i (April, 1962), 10–17. Copyright © 1962 by *Twentieth Century Literature*. Reprinted by permission of *Twentieth Century Literature, Inc.*

part of the very fabric of the play functioning within, as well as enlarging, its surface meaning.

On the simplest level *The Zoo Story* is concerned with human isolation. The world is a zoo "with everyone separated by bars from everyone else, the animals for the most part from each other, and always the people from the animals" (49)*; that is, men are not only separated from each other, but from their own basic animal natures (as Peter, one of "the people" is, until the end of the play, separated from his own animal nature).

The play opens upon Peter, who is seated on a bench in the park. As Albee tells us in his description of the dramatis personae, Peter is "neither fat nor gaunt, neither handsome nor homely." He is, in fact, in no way distinctive. Peter is the modern version, in middle-class stereotype, of Everyman. He reads the "right" books, lives on the "right" side of the park, has the average number of children, and the "right" Madison Avenue job. His is the New Yorker ad life to which most middle-class citizens, consciously or unconsciously, aspire. He blends perfectly into the brightly-packaged emptiness of the modern landscape. The "bars" which separate Peter from his own nature and from other people are the material goods and the prefabricated ideas with which he surrounds himself. He has himself carefully constructed his isolation.

Peter would prefer not to talk with Jerry but is too polite and too afraid of anyone's bad opinion, even Jerry's, to ignore him. Once engaged in conversation, he tries to avoid talking about any subject that has real relevance, anything that has roots penetrating the carefully prepared mask which he presents to the world, and even to himself. When Jerry, trying to establish some real contact with Peter, questions him about his having more children, he withdraws from the conversation, furious that Jerry might have spotted a chink in his armor.

> *Jerry.* And you're not going to have any more kids, are you?
> *Peter.* (a bit distantly) No. No more. (Then back and irksome) Why did you say that? How would you know that?
> *Jerry.* The way you cross your legs perhaps; something in the voice. Or maybe I'm just guessing. Is it your wife?
> *Peter.* (furious) That's none of your business. Do you understand? (18)

Peter, who hardly acknowledges his own physicality, is furious and frightened that a stranger should try to expose it.

* [Quotations in this article are from: Edward Albee, *The Zoo Story and Other Plays* (London: Jonathan Cape Ltd., 1962).—Ed.]

Although Peter, in spite of himself, becomes interested in Jerry's confessions, he is embarrassed by Jerry's candor. He would much prefer to steer the conversation to the safe, if shallow, waters of conventional small talk. He tries to restrict himself to talk about the weather or books. And the only time during the conversation that he feels comfortable, indeed expansive, is when he launches into a "canned" evaluation of the comparative merits of Marquand and Baudelaire, which Jerry, to his dismay, cuts short and dismisses as pretentious. Jerry disturbs Peter because he cannot easily be fit into any of Peter's neatly labelled pigeonholes.

> *Peter.* Oh, you live in the Village (this seems to enlighten Peter)
> *Jerry.* No, I don't . . .
> *Peter.* (almost pouting) Oh, I thought you lived in the Village.
> *Jerry.* What were you trying to do? Make sense out of things, bring order?
>   The old pigeonhole bit? (25)

Peter, then, is self-isolated. His life of things and prejudices protects him from himself and from the world. While it provides no gut-pleasures, neither does it allow for gut-pain. Peter's is a kind of middle-class stoicism. But while genuine stoicism raises a man above pleasure and pain, this middle-class variety protects by anaesthetizing him in the commonplace.

While Peter is one of the "people" who is separated from the animal in himself and others, Jerry is an animal (he knows his own nature) who fights separation from the other animals. In part his isolation is forced upon him. But in large measure it grows out of his need for truth. He is determined to discover the essential nature of the human condition. Therefore, he strips himself of goods, things, obvious relationships. He has a strong box without a lock, picture frames without pictures, and pornographic playing cards that remind him of the difference between love and sexual need. Deprived of the usual family relationships, he refuses either to sentimentalize them or to console himself for what he is with comforting justifications built upon memories of an unhappy childhood.

The same urge for truth that enables Jerry to know himself makes communication between him and the other animals almost impossible, for the truth about human relationships that Jerry recognizes is that men are islands irrevocably cut off from one another. Contact is from time to time made, but always with great pain and difficulty and never with any assurance that it can be sustained. Jerry tells Peter what he has learned about human relations in his tale of Jerry and The Dog.

Being cut off from one another, we fear, and fearing, we hate with an unreasoning hatred any creature who threatens to invade that little area of the world that provides us with security. The dog attacks Jerry only when Jerry tries to enter the house, "whenever I came in; but never when I went out. . . . I could pack up and live in the street for all the dog cared." (37) The dog considers the house his domain just as Peter, later in the play, considers the park bench which he has appropriated his. Both Peter and the dog are willing to fight to the death any invader of their territories.

We cannot buy love or understanding, nor can we establish real contact by any easy means. Jerry bribes the dog with hamburgers but this gains him only the tactical advantage of a few extra minutes to race up the stairs before the dog attacks him.

> Poor bastard, he never learned that the moment he took to smile before he went for me gave me time enough to get out of range. But there he was, malevolence with an erection waiting. (39)

The dog reflects with deadly accuracy all of the qualities which Jerry finds in the animals of his own species (his parents, for instance, or the landlady): hatred, lust, smiling exploitation, and treachery. Jerry and the dog stand in antithetical relation to one another. They are a pair of armed enemies sizing each other up, waiting to spring or to outmaneuver one another. Theirs is a perfect model of most human relationships, as Jerry sees them. Any superficial attempt at conciliation merely lulls for a moment the enmity which is caused by their isolation and fear.

To establish contact one must reach below the surface to the level of pain and pleasure, to the animal core. "I have learned," Jerry says, "that neither kindness or cruelty, independent of each other creates any effect beyond themselves; and I have learned that the two combined, together, at the same time are the teaching emotion." One must reach into the realm where emotions themselves are not sharply differentiated. But, as Jerry explains, even the flash of understanding that can result from such a contact gives no assurance that the contact can endure for more than an instant. "And what is gained is loss. And what has been the result; the dog and I have attained a compromise: more of a bargain, really. We neither love nor hurt because we do not try to reach each other."

Jerry applies the knowledge he has gained from his contact with the dog in trying to establish contact with Peter. Realizing that Peter cannot be drawn out of his tough shell with talk, that words when they do penetrate Peter's surface, merely cause him to throw up further barriers to contact, Jerry tries to touch Peter beneath this consciously preserved surface. He begins by tickling Peter. Tickling, being a pleasure-pain experience, perfectly implements Jerry's theory that the teaching emotion involves cruelty and kindness combined. It must perforce elicit a primitive, animal response. The effect upon Peter of the tickling is startling and immediate. It enables him, for the first time, to relax his grip upon the shield that his "perfect" life provides.

> *Peter.* Oh hee, hee, hee. I must go. I . . . hee, hee, hee. After all, stop, stop, hee, hee, hee, after all the parakeets will be getting dinner ready soon. And the cats are setting the table. Stop, stop . . . and we're having . . .
> (Jerry stops tickling Peter but the combination of the tickling and his own mad whimsy has Peter laughing almost hysterically. As his laughter continues, then subsides, Jerry watches him with a curious, fixed smile.)

Peter goes on laughing and Jerry reminds him that something has happened at the zoo about which Peter is curious.

> *Peter.* Ah ha, ha, the what? Oh, yes, the zoo. Well, I had my own zoo there for a moment with . . . hee, hee, the parakeets getting dinner ready. . . . Oh my, I don't know what happened to me. (48)

The teaching, pleasure-pain emotion has enabled Peter to see clearly for a brief moment the emptiness of his life, a life in which cats, children, wife, and parakeets are interchangeable because they are all merely props whose function it is to disguise nothingness and isolation.

After he has established this first contact, which is comparable to the contact he had achieved with the dog in that its purpose was to enlighten, Jerry goads Peter into a fight. In forcing Peter to fight for the park bench, Jerry is once again challenging Peter's attachment to material things that are in themselves without value to him. Peter responds to the invasion of his "property" with the same ferocity that the dog has shown. Peter is again forced by Jerry to respond at the animal level, like a savage fighting for a bone. Finally, Jerry makes Peter kill him. Peter, we assume, can never again exist on the surface level, can never again avoid contact with himself. And Jerry has at last established a contact that must endure, for Peter will never be able to forget a man he has killed.

It is within the naturalism that we have been discussing that the play's symbolism operates. The symbols are large and are, as I said earlier, traditional Christian symbols. There is Jerry, or Jesus, a thirty-year-old outcast whose purpose is to establish contact "with God who is a colored queen who wears a kimono and plucks his eyebrows, who is a woman who cries with determination behind her closed door . . . with God, who I'm told, turned his back on the whole thing some time ago. . . ." And there is Peter, St. Peter, an average worldling who is stripped by the irresistible Jerry or his material goods and led toward a revelation of truth. So carefully constructed and maintained is the symbolic pattern that it skirts being allegory. What preserves it as symbol is that its function in the naturalistic design of the play is never lost. Let us examine the symbolic pattern more closely and observe its relation to the pattern of meaning we have discussed.

Jerry, when we meet him, has lived for a short time in a rooming house on the West Side. The inhabitants of the rooming house are a Negro homosexual, a Puerto Rican family, and a woman who cries incessantly. They are, in effect, the outcasts, the doomed, the "least of these." The gate keepers (the word is Jerry's) of the rooming house are a foul woman and a dog, "a black monster of a beast: an oversized head, tiny, tiny ears and eyes. . . . The dog is black, all black except for the bloodshot eyes." (36) The description immediately identifies the dog as Cerberus, the monster, all black with flaming eyes, who guards Hell. The drunken, lewd woman whose affection for the dog is almost maternal adds a further dimension to the allusion for we recognize the pair as Milton's Sin and Death. The symbol is again reinforced and expanded when Jerry throws poisoned meat to the dog in his effort to gain safe passage, for this is an unmistakable allusion to the myth in which Theseus throws drugged honey-cakes to Cerberus to gain entrance to the Underworld. The West Side rooming house, then, is Hell and Jerry's adventures with the dog symbolize the mythical hero's or God's descent into Hell. We see here Albee's method of symbolism. He chooses old symbols, that carry with them a wealth of meaning but that yet do no violence to the naturalistic surface of his play.

To go on to the identification of Jerry as Jesus—when the landlady asks him to pray for her sick dog, Jerry replies, "Madam, I have myself to pray for, the colored queen, the Puerto Rican family, the person whom I have never seen, the women who cries behind the closed door, and the rest of the people in all the rooming houses everywhere." This modernized Messiah first identifies himself with the outcasts and the afflicted and then assumes responsibility for them.

From time to time Albee gives the audience broad clues to his symbolic equivalents so that his meaning cannot be mistaken. For example, when Jerry is revealing to Peter the nature of the human condition by means of the parable of the dog (for that, indeed, is what the Tale of Jerry and the Dog is, a parable), he uses, in broad parody, a Biblical locution, "And it came to pass that the beast was deathly ill." Or again, after Jerry-Jesus has harrowed Hell (that is, gained entrance into the rooming house and assumed responsibility for its inmates) and is ready for the job of salvation, he must come to Peter by a very curious route.

> . . . I took the subway down to the Village so I could walk all the way up Fifth Avenue to the zoo. It's one of those things a person has to do; sometimes a person has to come a very long distance out of his way to come back a short distance correctly. (25)

The journey downtown and up, at the end of which lies the salvation of a man is, of course, Christ's descent into Hell and Resurrection which are necessary before the Redemption can begin.

Peter refuses Jerry-Jesus' message when it appears in the parable of the dog. He first deliberately resists understanding, then he pretends that he has not understood, and finally he covers his ears to escape the truth that has been revealed to him.

> *Jerry.* Oh, come on now, Peter, tell me what you think.
> *Peter.* (numb) I . . . I don't understand what . . . I don't think I . . . (Now almost tearfully) Why did you tell me all of this?
> *Jerry.* Why not?
> *Peter.* I DON'T UNDERSTAND.
> *Jerry.* (Furious, but whispering) That's a lie.
> *Peter.* No, no, it's not.
> *Jerry.* (Quietly) I tried to explain to you as I went along. I went slowly; it all had to do with—
> *Peter.* I DON'T WANT TO HEAR ANY MORE. (44, 45)

Jerry's parable, like the Gospels, is spoken slowly and framed in the simplest terms. But, like the Gospels, it is rejected by Everyman who pretends not to understand, who pleads confusion, and who finally flees from the responsibility that understanding would demand. Jerry's truth cannot be conveyed in words.

In tickling Peter and causing him for a second to lose his grip, to penetrate the falsity of his life, Jerry is, in effect, symbolically stripping Peter of his worldly goods and causing him to "follow" him. Once

Peter has, even whimsically, questioned the "happiness" of having the right life, the right family, the right pets, he has taken the first steps toward his salvation. He has taken the first step in a journey that will lead him to the realization of what it is like to be essentially human and to be an outcast. Finally, realizing the futility of trying to reach Peter with words, realizing too the fragility of the vision of truth that has flashed before Peter's mind during the tickling, Jerry dies for Peter. He dies to save Peter's soul from death by spiritual starvation. Peter will be forced by Jerry's death to know himself and to feel kinship with the outcasts for whom Jerry has prayed.

In the dialogue of the death scene Albee again makes his allusions very broad. In the instant before Jerry decides to impale himself upon the knife there is a suggestion of his momentary indecision, followed by acceptance of his fate which he declares in a spoken resolution.

> *Peter.* I'll give you one last chance to get out of here and leave me alone.
> (He holds the knife with a firm hand but far in front of him, not to attack, but to defend.)
> *Jerry.* (Sighs heavily) So be it. (59)

This decision to accept death for man's salvation, with its air of the culmination of a foreordained pattern, is the modernized scene at Gethsemane. Again the somewhat archaic locution strengthens the allusion.

In the death scene itself the allusion is so broad that it becomes ironic. Peter's calling "Oh, my God" operates so well on both symbolistic and naturalistic level that the one level becomes an ironic commentary upon the other. The words are, of course, the very words we feel we would utter were we caught in so horrible a situation, so that they are naturalistically "true" and yet, ironically, on the symbolistic level it *is* God, the God he has slain, whom Peter is addressing.

> *Peter.* Oh my God, Oh my God, Oh my God.
> *Jerry.* (Jerry is dying, but now his expression seems to change. His features relax, and while his voice varies, sometimes wrenched with pain, for the most part, he seems removed from his dying.) Thank you, Peter, I mean that now; thank you very much. I came unto you and you have comforted me, dear Peter.
> *Peter.* (Almost fainting) Oh my God.
> *Jerry.* You'd better go now. Somebody might come by and you don't want to be here when anyone comes.
> *Peter.* (Does not move, but begins to weep.) Oh my God. Oh my God.

Jerry. (His eyes still closed, he shakes his head and speaks: a combination of scornful mimicry and supplication.) Oh . . . my . . . God.   (62)

The allusion is perfectly sustained and in the mouth of a skillful actor Peter's repetition of the phrase contains infinite variety, expressing varying degrees of awareness. This Crucifixion scene is also underscored by Peter's betrayal when, taking his book and leaving the dying Jerry, he, in effect, denies that "he knows the man."

What Albee has written in *The Zoo Story* is a modern Morality play. The theme is the centuries old one of human isolation and salvation through sacrifice. Man in his natural state is alone, a prisoner of Self. If he succumbs to fear he enforces his isolation in denying it. Pretending that he is not alone, he surrounds himself with things and ideas that bolster the barrier between himself and all other creatures. The good man first takes stock of himself. Once he has understood his condition, realized his animality and the limitations imposed upon him by Self, he is driven to prove his kinship with all other things and creatures, "with a bed, with a cockroach, with a mirror. . . ." (The progression that Jerry describes is Platonic.) In proving this kinship he is extending his boundaries, defying Self, proving his humanity, since the kinship of all nature can be recognized only by the animal who has within him a spark of divinity. He finds at last, if he has been completely truthful in his search, that the only way in which he can smash the walls of his isolation and reach his fellow creatures is by an act of love, a sacrifice, so great that it altogether destroys the self that imprisons him, that it kills him. Albee, in recreating this theme, has used a pattern of symbolism that is an immensely expanded allusion to the story of Christ's sacrifice. But the symbolism is not outside of the story which he has to tell, which is the story of *modern* man and *his* isolation and hope for salvation. He uses the allusion to support his own story. He has chosen traditional Christian symbols, I think, not because they are tricky attention-getters, but because the sacrifice of Christ is perhaps the most effective way that the story has been told in the past.

The Death of Bessie Smith

by Gilbert Debusscher

. . . On April 21, 1960, [Albee] presented *The Death of Bessie Smith* at the Schlosspark Theater in Berlin where he had achieved his first success. This was another success, and he was henceforward on his way to becoming a celebrated American in Europe. . . .

In eight scenes without interruption, the changes of time are only indicated by very brief blackouts. There is no plot properly speaking, no development of a situation, but rather the evocation of two parallel worlds. One is that of the Nurse in charge of admissions in a Memphis, Tennessee, hospital. At home, she is the target of the peevish hostility of her father, an embittered and impotent old man who reproaches her for her long nocturnal sessions in the car of her friend, the Intern. She feels only a physical attraction for the Intern, scorning the flimsy idealism which tempts him to go to Spain to fight Franco, deriding his financial condition, exasperated by his superior airs. She has discovered an ideal scapegoat in the person of a mulatto Orderly who is trying to thrust himself into a society where there is no place for Negroes, without disturbing the peace. This universe of illusion, frustration, and lies runs parallel to the tragic destiny of Bessie Smith, the black singer, who dies as the result of an automobile accident for lack of help (she has been refused admittance to another all-white hospital).

In the last scene, Jack, Bessie's friend and the driver of the automobile, bursts into the admitting room where the Nurse has just vented her frustrations in a long sadistic monologue. While the Intern runs out to the damaged car where Bessie Smith lies, Jack describes the catastrophe and the rejection which he encountered at the first hospital. His narrative is equal in horror to the parable of Jerry in *The Zoo Story:*

"*The Death of Bessie Smith*" (editor's title). From "The Playwright in the Making" in *Edward Albee: Tradition and Renewal* by Gilbert Debusscher, pp. 21–30. Translated by Mrs. Anne D. Williams. Copyright © 1967 by American Studies Centre, Brussels. Reprinted by permission of American Studies Centre, Brussels.

> . . . and I said . . . I said, Honey, we have crashed . . . you all right?
> (*His face contorts*) And I looked . . . and the door was all pushed in
> . . . she was caught there . . . where the door had pushed in . . . her
> right side, crushed into the torn door, the door crushed into her right
> side. . . . BESSIE! BESSIE! . . . (*More to the Nurse, now*) . . . but
> ma'am . . . her arm . . . her right arm . . . was torn off . . . almost
> torn off from her shoulder . . . and there was blood . . . SHE WAS
> BLEEDING SO . . . !

When the Intern returns, violently affected, Jack admits that he had
known Bessie was dead even as he drove her from one hospital to the
other. The Nurse bursts into hysterical laughter; the Intern slaps
her and goes out as the Orderly murmurs, "I never heard of such a
thing . . . bringing a dead woman here like that . . . I don't know
what people can be thinking of sometimes . . ."

The most obvious theme of this play is doubtless that suggested by
the situation—racism. Bessie Smith in Albee's work becomes the victim,
not of an automobile accident, but of the intolerance raging in the
South. The author has taken care not to limit his subject to the
anecdote and to generalize his argument. Racism appears in the play
at three different levels. First it is manifest in the simple withholding
of aid to Bessie Smith. But this aspect, if it is the most brutal and the
most eloquent, is held to an undercurrent through most of the play,
being directly expressed in barely three of the shorter scenes. Moreover,
Albee explicitly refuses to personalize the victim: he never shows Bessie
Smith to us. It might be argued that by using her name he necessarily
restricted his message to a specific case. But the singer died in 1937 and
the play was written in 1959—that is to say, at a time when the circumstances of her accident and death had long formed a Bessie Smith
legend. Thus the name no longer referred to a single person, but to a
while race of pariahs, of the disinherited. The language touches on the
same problem in a network of allusions, images and remarks which,
in isolation, would have minimal effect, but which combine to establish
more surely than a long description the racist climate of the South,
the atmosphere permeated with prejudice, cruelty and hatred. At one
time the Father fulminates against "those goddam nigger records"
which aggravate his headaches. At another the Nurse amuses herself
by humiliating the Orderly, assigning him degrading errands, reminding him that the needs of their Negro patients come second in the
hospital's priority to the whim of their honored patient, the Mayor
(who is undergoing treatment for his hemorrhoids). Again, the Intern

ironically taunts the Nurse about the lynchings and other horrible punishments reserved for Negroes: ". . . orderlies you may burn at will, unless you have other plans for them. . . ."

In the relationship between the Nurse and the Orderly, Albee has found another—and perhaps the most effective—level of meaning. Here he recovers the evocative power of *The Zoo Story* when he draws for us a Negro who has become auto-racist. The character is at once pathetic and repellent, a monster and a martyr. His legitimate desire to find his place in the sun is transformed into an obsequious opportunism: he endures any sarcasm, wounding remark or disgusting duty. He tries to please everyone and succeeds in isolating himself from all. Banished and disgraced by his race, he is the target and laughingstock of his betters, the whites. The Nurse even suggests (and here Albee's imagination is truly superlative) that in order to escape his condition he spends his evening soaking bleach into his skin.

But the Negro himself is only criticized to the extent that the criticism also applies to the white society which conditions him. In the last scene, he is leaning with his back to the wall—a symbolic posture —but it is an empty being, an automaton without a soul, who speaks. He is at this point so estranged from his world that the death of a black woman signifies less to him, who should be the first one touched by it, than to the Nurse or the Intern. Albee has been able to create here an impressive image of all those who have let themselves be convinced that it is shameful to be born black. But his goal is primarily to brand those who have done the convincing. With *The Death of Bessie Smith* Albee made his contribution to the activities of northern intellectuals on behalf of racial equality. His art became the means to criticize and denounce a situation to which, as an American, he is particularly sensitive. Through an individual history he evokes profound causes, the roots of the evil, and powerfully cries out his indignation:

> . . . while the incident, itself, was brawling at me, and while the characters I had elected to carry the tale were wrestling it from me, I discovered I was, in fact, writing about something at the same time slightly removed from and more pertinent to what I had imagined. . . . I know only that the play, printed here, is, whatever its failings or successes may be, most exactly what I had to say on the matter.

Apart from racism, certain preoccupations recurrent in the entire body of his work reappear in this play. The most important is unarguably the sexual metaphor, which expresses the fundamental prob-

lem of the main characters. The Father's reproaches to the Nurse
clearly exceed simple paternal concern. Their dialogue has an undercurrent of latent jealousy which renders the second scene a lovers'
quarrel rather than a parental lecture. The Nurse's attitude toward her
father remains negative; it is nevertheless in the aftermath of this conversation that she rejects the Intern's proposals. Later also, while she
refuses to participate in the old man's delusions of grandeur, she
defends him against the critical whimsies of the Intern. The attachment between father and daughter is therefore the more constricting
as, for her at least, it is subconscious and only indirectly expressed. The
theme of incestuous love introduced here in half-tone reappears in
The American Dream and above all in *Who's Afraid of Virginia Woolf?*

The war of the sexes, however, finds fullness of expression in the
exchanges between the Nurse and the Intern. What begins in light,
flirtatious conversation degenerates immediately into moral combat,
the intensity of which is a measure of the protagonists' frustrations.
Their progressively unleashed violence expresses itself in a harshness
of language rarely heard in the theater. The technical precision of the
terms soon gives way to much more evocative images and innuendo
which have an unfortunate tendency to pornographic obsession; the
lewd vocabulary easily equals in vulgarity Martha's in *Who's Afraid of
Virginia Wolf?* And like Martha in the first half of that play, the Nurse
emerges victorious from the verbal combat. She becomes the circus lion-
tamer armed with a whip, or the instrument of wild-West justice:
"Honey, your neck is in the *noose* . . . and I have a whip . . . and
I'll set the horse from under you . . . when it pleases me"—or the
triumphant femme fatale, the devouring virago of Strindberg:

> *Intern.* Now that he [the Orderly] is back from one errand, are you
> planning to send me on another?
> *Nurse.* (*Smiling wickedly*) Yeah . . . I think I'd like that . . . keep both
> of you jumping. I *would* like coffee, and I *would* like you to get it for
> me. So why don't you just trot right across the hall and get me some?
> And I like it good and hot . . . and strong . . .
> *Intern.* . . . and black . . . ?

The ambiguity of the Intern's last question is all the more evident as
the Negro Orderly remains on stage with the Nurse. It is on him that
she turns to take out her rage, her perverse imagination suggesting
gratuitous tortures to inflict on him. But here again racial prejudice is
reinforced by an exacerbated sexuality. In the scene where her hysteria
makes her look forward to the happy day when she will be able to

make these two puppets dance—the one whom she despises racially, and the other whom she scorns financially—she equates the two in terms of their use to her. Freudians would certainly detect here a repressed and subconscious sexual desire for the Orderly, whom she drowns in abuse but who fascinates her. The attraction felt by the white is a manifestation of the familiar southern perversity that used Negroes willingly for sexual satisfaction then projected the blame onto them—a point that Albee makes strongly here since it is a white woman who is attracted to a black man, a notion so shocking to Southerners as to be blasphemous.

The false idealism of the young doctor is nothing but a feebly satisfying response to his sexual frustrations. His intimate relationship with the Nurse consists of

> . . . fifteen minutes or so of . . . of tantalizing preliminary love play ending in an infuriating and inconclusive wrestling match, during which you hiss of the . . . the liberties I should not take, and I sound the horn once or twice accidentally with my elbow . . . (*She giggles at this*) . . . and, finally, in my beat-up car, in front of your father's beat-up house . . . a kiss of searing intensity . . . a hand in the right place . . . briefly . . . and your hasty departure within.

Against this humiliating frustration he seeks refuge in an anti-Franco leftism.

In short, the theme of sexuality takes on the aspect of a war of the sexes which Albee might have found in Strindberg. It is to be noted also that by contrast to the frustrated and gesticulating marionettes who are the Nurse and the Intern, the relationship only lightly sketched between Jack and Bessie, the most human characters of the play, seems more normal and balanced. We may see here, slightly modified, a favorite theme of Tennessee Williams: the Anglo-Saxons of the South are degenerated to the point of becoming prey to their passions, while the Negroes (aliens, recent immigrants in Williams) have a vitality and human completeness by virtue of which these problems resolve themselves naturally.

The third important theme of *The Death of Bessie Smith* is that of illusion, of the life-lie. Suggested in *The Zoo Story*, it is here further developed, foreshadowing *Who's Afraid of Virginia Woolf?* where the problem acquires central importance. All the characters in *The Death of Bessie Smith* are out of touch with reality. Everyone has, in the words of the Nurse, "a pretty hard time reconciling himself to things as they are." Everyone, consequently, has composed a world of dreams in which he tries to survive and to which he has secured himself as if to a life-buoy. The Father, deteriorated, as much physically as morally, his helplessness symbolized by an ineffectual cane, has fastened on the idea of an illusory past grandeur; now he pretends to a close friendship with the mayor. The Negro Orderly, a pariah who denies his birthright incessantly, believes that one day he will have done forever with carrying bedpans for white patients and bearing his superiors' taunts. The Intern, a beginning doctor in a second-rate hospital in the deep South, dreams of noble deeds and a glorious career. But his mediocre job serves him as a pretext for not setting out for Spain to fight Franco. Jack, the friend of Bessie Smith, has his own dream— a second chance for Bessie, a return to success and fame symbolized by a trip to New York, to a mythical *North* where all men are equal. The Nurse also seeks to escape the familial, economic, emotional and sexual frustrations of her situation: she deludes herself that she is a member of an important family with good prospects for marrying above her condition.

Absurdly, destiny, another guise of Gregers Werle, arrives to smash their illusions and reveal their tragic imperfections. Bessie Smith dies in a car accident. The new career Jack dreams of ends before it can begin; the young doctor's willingness to act runs afoul of ineluctable death. The Orderly dooms himself by his refusal to help and understand his Negro brethren. The Nurse also seems to triumph, but her victory is a death comparable to Jerry's in *The Zoo Story*, since she annihilates the man she is attracted to; nor can she wholeheartedly participate in her father's pretense of aristocracy.

The final message is as despairing as in the gloomiest plays of Strindberg and the bitterest of Ibsen. In *The Wild Duck* after a series of illustrations of the life-lie, the Norwegian dramatist has Dr. Relling draw a pragmatic lesson which finally reveals the truth to Gregers Werle, the instrument of the drama. But we would search in vain in *The Death of Bessie Smith* for a protagonist capable of extracting meaning from the jazz-singer's death. Not one shows even the first dawning consciousness of the absurdity of his life and the tragedy of death. On this philosophical pessimism is superimposed a social tragedy, already painted on a noble scale by Tennessee Williams—the decay of southern society, the shameful anachronism in the heart of America. This image of a dying society is underlined by the symbolism of the setting sun, which gives the whole play its nostalgic aura. The absurdity of individual existence is thus made perceptible in a social context and a symbolic atmosphere which extend not only to an entire generation but to the succession of generations which form a civilization.

Consequently, what holds our attention is less the characters themselves than the historical and metaphysical drama which they act out before us. These characters *en situation* are charged with demonstrating the absurdity of a particular society—but also the absurdity of the human condition in general. Proofs are hardly needed of this reduction of characters to abstractions. In the manner of Strindberg and the German expressionists, Albee has given names only to Bessie Smith, her friend Jack, and their bar acquaintance, Bernie. All three are authentic Negroes who suffer, hope and die because they have been born black. He establishes a contrast with the other characters, who are only identified by their function. The Orderly, who has disowned his essence, has also lost his name. In contrast with the other Negroes in the play, he is only the anonymous "orderly." In a Strindbergian expressionistic fashion the characters also have an aspect of caricature: the Nurse is the female vampire who ushers in the gallery of Albee's destructive women; the young doctor is only an ineffectual idealist; the Orderly is an Uncle Tom, preoccupied with offending no one; the Father is all helpless spite. Opposite them is Bessie Smith, an invisible presence who paradoxically seems more vivid by her pathetic effort to "come back," more authentic in her stupefied condition, more pitiable and human because of her severed arm, her bruised flesh, her spilled blood—more important finally by her very destitution and death. Through the intentional irony, the marionettes one sees grow pale before the humanity of the one who never appears.

It has been said that the play suffers from a structural deficiency, that the two parallel plots only coalesce at the moment when the play is ended, that the two actions are integrated little if at all. It is obvious that this is not a well-made play to which one can apply the criteria of realistic theater; the schematic characterization, the cinematographic cutting, the suggested setting, the symbolic lighting, bring this play closer to the German expressionistic theater. To confront the spectator with a shocking situation which will jar his indifference, Albee employs a dual device: the death of Bessie Smith, the result of absurd racial prejudice, suddenly throws a revealing light on the vacuousness of the characters, their existences and their hopes, and on the desperate absurdity of the human condition. Even if we refuse to concede Albee's structural success, the human situations which he has created, the evocative language, the vigorously ironic dialogue and the particularly nervous rhythm make the play an arresting work.

Gerald Weales said in 1962 that *The Death of Bessie Smith* is a thematic and formal exception in the works of Albee.[1] On the contrary, it seems to me that the play is part of a continuous development. The playwright passes from the mitigated naturalism of *The Zoo Story*, through a period of expressionistic experimentation, to the ironic surrealism of *The Sandbox* and *The American Dream*. On the other hand, the themes of the battle of the sexes and the life-lie recall the preceding play and foreshadow *Who's Afraid of Virginia Woolf?* The character of the Nurse, with her frustrations, her paternal attachment, her scorn of the other sex, her hysterical determination to destroy what she loves, and her intense vulgarity, is a prefiguration of Martha. This play elaborates a portrait of Woman worthy of Strindberg which is repeated in each of the later plays. . . .

1 Gerald Weales, *American Drama Since World War II* (Harcourt, Brace & World, 1962), p. 219.

Who's Afraid of Edward Albee?

by Richard Schechner

> The American theatre should experiment, for admittedly
> it is the special privilege of any youngish man or land to ex-
> periment, to fail or, after blundering, to succeed. But if to
> experiment independently is acting boldly, to pose as experi-
> menting while depending on an elder hand is of course really
> not experimenting at all.
>
> —Gordon Craig, 1928

The premiere of Edward Albee's first Broadway hit raises distinct
problems for the American theatre. Albee is grown up now and he is
no longer sheltered by that lovely excuse of inadequacy, "promising
young playwright." *Who's Afraid of Virginia Woolf?* announces
Albee's arrival and the New York critics, hungry for a king, have welcomed him to our theatre royalty, enthroning Albee next to O'Neill,
Miller, and Williams. This joke would be unworthy of comment except
that Albee's coronation—far from being a happy event—uncovers a
running sore in our theatre.

What makes Albee run? It can't simply be his salaciousness, his
dirty jokes, his ability to wisecrack as glibly as Lenny Bruce. These
things contribute to his popularity of course, for no road is easier to
run than that sexy highway blazed over a half-century ago. But it would
be merely smug to condemn our theatre this way, and then sit back and
wait for the return of the Roman circus with its exciting sadism and its
diverting coital games. No; Albee runs because we see in his work a reflection of a sentimental view of ourselves, a view which pleases us. Like
children or never-quite-reformed Puritans who cannot forget Jonathan
Edwards we enjoy thinking of ourselves as "naughty," and we eagerly
exaggerate our naughtiness into hard vices and our vices into per-

versities. Oh, if we only could play "humiliate the host" or "hump the hostess" as do the heroes of *Virginia Woolf*; if only our lives were truly *that* decadent! Albee gratifies an adolescent culture which likes to think of itself as decadent.

We want to believe that we are living in the last days, that the world is falling in on our heads, that only our sickest illusions are able to offer us any reason for living. Everyone wants to be Nero watching Rome burn. To attend the last orgy, to be part of it, this is a comfortable and exciting escape from reality—the child's way out. Albee's characters, like the playwright himself, suffer from arrested development. They play the game of decadence, just as he plays the game of creativity. There is no real, hard bedrock of suffering in *Virginia Woolf* —it is all illusory, depending upon a "child" who never was born: a gimmick, a trick, a trap. And there is no solid creative suffering in the writer who meanders through a scene stopping here and there for the sake of a joke or an easy allusion that *almost* fits.

But even more, the values of *Virginia Woolf* are perverse and dangerous. Self-pity, drooling, womb-seeking weakness, the appeal to a transcendent "god" who is no God, the persistent escape into morbid fantasy—all these things are probably too close to our *imagined* picture of ourselves. It is the game of the child who thinks he is being persecuted, who dreams up all kinds of outrages, and who concludes finally that his parents found him one day on the doorstep. Albee wants us to indulge in this same game, this cheap hunt for love; he wants us to point to the stage and simper: "Oooo, there we are! How pitiable, how terrible!" The danger is that Albee may succeed; we are on the verge of becoming the silly role we are playing.

I much prefer Gelber where junk is junk and the connection is real. In Gelber—as in O'Neill, Williams, and Miller—there is at least a sincerity, an honesty. But Albee makes dishonesty a virtue, perversion a joke, adultery a simple party game. In honest play-writing if man is mocked he is mocked before God, before the human condition; in Albee's play man is mocked before Oswald Spengler. Sartre once described the life of bad faith as a living lie—of actually believing an untruth and then acting on that false belief. Albee is not conscious of his own phoniness, nor of the phoniness of his work. But he has posed so long that his pose has become part of the fabric of his creative life; he *is* his own lie. If *Virginia Woolf* is a tragedy it is of that unique kind rarely seen: a tragedy which transcends itself, a tragedy which is bad theatre, bad literature, bad taste—but which *believes* its own lies with such conviction that it indicts the society which creates it and accepts it. *Virginia Woolf* is a ludicrous play; but the joke is on all of us.

The upsetting thing—the deeply upsetting thing—is that American theatre-goers and their critics have welcomed this phony play and its writer as the harbinger of a new wave in the American theatre. The American theatre, our theatre, is so hungry, so voracious, so corrupt, so morally blind, so perverse that *Virginia Woolf* is a success. I am outraged at a theatre and an audience that accepts as a masterpiece an insufferably long play with great pretensions that lacks intellectual size, emotional insight, and dramatic electricity. I'm tired of play-long "metaphors"—such as the illusory child of *Virginia Woolf*—which are neither philosophically, psychologically, nor poetically valid. I'm tired of plays that are badly plotted and turgidly written being excused by such palaver as "organic unity" or "inner form." I'm tired of morbidity and sexual perversity which are there only to titillate an impotent and homosexual theatre and audience. I'm tired of Albee.

Genet can raise sexual perversion to the level of ontological speculation—he is a poet and a mighty intellect. Beckett can transform static dramatic situations into valid metaphors for man's condition—he, too, is a poet and a mighty intellect. Albee can only follow meagerly and blindly in their path, patching together several of their insights and devices over the thinly disguised skeleton of Eugene O'Neill. I am ashamed of a theatre which welcomes Albee's new play as a classic, because this means only that we are starving for heroes and kings and will pay almost any price, including our own theatrical self-respect, our self-respect as artists and citizens, for them. *Virginia Woolf* is doubtlessly a classic: a classic example of bad taste, morbidity, plotless naturalism, misrepresentation of history, American society, philosophy, and psychology. There is in the play an ineluctable urge to escape reality and its concomitant responsibilities by crawling back into the womb, or bathroom, or both.

A dear friend of mine wrote to me that *Virginia Woolf* gnawed at her, and that such a play must have something to it—that it could not be ignored. That's right—there is no way in which we can ignore danger or disease. But it is not right therefore to welcome the plague into our midst. We must not ignore what Albee represents and portends, either for our theatre or for our society. The lie of his work is the lie of our theatre and the lie of America. The lie of decadence must be fought. It is no accident that the other side of the coin—the lie of painless goodness—also had a fine run on Broadway as it was portrayed in Robert Bolt's comforting paean to nostalgia, *A Man for All Seasons*. We must fight both lies. But Albee's is more dangerous —for it is a lie in current usage these days, and one which is likely to have an infective and corrosive influence on our theatre.

Why So Afraid?

by *Alan Schneider*

Let's start by admitting that I'm prejudiced: I directed Edward
Albee's play, and I've been reading TDR for years. Normally, I don't
believe in responding to bad notices of plays I've worked on (or good
ones either); but I am outraged and ashamed that the Editor of our
leading theatrical quarterly has made so sweeping a series of statements concerning Albee's sincerity of intention, his character, and his
talent; it is not possible for me to stomach without protest an indictment of Edward Albee's work as a "lie" and a "plague," an indictment
as fundamentally false as those earlier ones, in less responsible quarters,
which labeled Samuel Beckett a "hoax" and Harold Pinter a "pretentious fake."

The right of the Editor—or anyone else—not to like or agree with
or even to understand *Who Afraid of Virginia Woolf?* is unquestioned.
Some of my best friends don't care for it though, as with the Editor's
example, the play continues to gnaw at them long after they have seen
it. There are also a few who write me notes or call me up in the
middle of the night to tell me how special they think it is, how much
it has affected their thinking, their emotions, and their faith in the
possibility of theatre. (Although the Editor states categorically that "it
lacks intellectual size, emotional insight, and dramatic electricity.")
Not all of them are psychotics, reactionaries, or homosexuals.

If I follow the Editor's general thesis, it contains several major
points: that comparing Albee to such elder statesmen as O'Neill,
Miller and Williams is sacrilege and a "joke"; that Albee's writing
is primarily a dirty joke, sentimentalized to fit in with our concepts of
"naughtiness" and "decadence"; that his work is based on gimmicks
but lacks any real substance; that his values are morbid, perverted,
imitative; and that those values (through the popular and critical suc-

"Why So Afraid?" by Alan Schneider. From *Tulane Drama Review*, VII, iii
(1963), 10–13. Copyright © 1963 by *Tulane Drama Review*. Reprinted by permission
of *The Drama Review*.

cess of *Virginia Woolf*) threaten to engulf and further destroy our theatre.

Without attempting to enthrone Albee alongside anyone (though I personally admire him above all other Americans now writing for the stage), or to hail *Virginia Woolf* as a classic of the modern theatre (which I have no doubt it will become), I would only state that, in my experience, a more honest or moral (in the true sense) playwright does not exist—unless it be Samuel Beckett. To blame Albee for the "sickness" of his subject matter is like blaming the world's ashcans on the creator of Nagg and Nell—which has been done. And if what Albee is doing is giving us a "sentimentalized" view of ourselves rather than one as harshly and starkly unsentimental as any I know, why didn't those theatre party ladies buy it up ahead of time as they do all those other technicolor postcards which pass for plays? Or is Albee not rather dedicated to smashing that rosy view, shocking us with the truth of our present-day behavior and thought, striving to purge us into an actual confrontation with reality? Anyone who has read any portion of any play he has ever written surely must sense the depth of his purpose and recognize, to some extent, the power of the talent which is at his disposal; certainly no intelligent, aware individual today can fail to recognize somewhere in Albee's characters and moods the stirring of his own viscera, the shadow of his own self-knowledge.

If the child in *Virginia Woolf* is merely a "gimmick," then so is the wild duck, the cherry orchard, that streetcar with the special name, even our old elusive friend Godot. But Albee's play is not about the child—just as *Godot* is not about Godot but about the waiting for him—but about the people who have had to create him as a "beanbag" or crutch for their own insufficiencies and failures, and now are left to find their own way, if there is to be a way, free of him. If truth and illusion are not exactly original themes, any more than they were for O'Neill, the test is not *what* but *how* and how specifically the writer illuminates the immediacy of human life. If Albee's particular choice is more lacking in plot than our editor wishes, its reality is based upon a classic simplicity, a contemporary feeling unmatched in our theatre, a musical economy—in spite of its length—and an ability to hold and shatter his audience.

What baffles me is why the Editor is making such a fuss. Is Western civilization actually in danger because both Howard Taubman and Walter Kerr managed to agree that *Virginia Woolf*—with all its faults —represents a major writing talent in our theatre and should be seen

by people who consider themselves serious theatre-goers? (Why, even
Bob Brustein had kind words to say about Albee this time, including
something about his having borrowed from the Greeks.) Would the
American theatre be better off, would it be less voracious, corrupt,
morally blind, and perverse, had the play never been written or presented? Would the Editor have been happier about life had the play
failed, i.e. echoed the verdict of the *New York Daily News* and *Mirror,*
those two shining Galahads of democratic journalism, which shared
his opinion that it was filthy, corrupt, gangrenous, and should immediately be withdrawn lest it contaminate the pure atmosphere of
the society which they represented.

That TDR is against the voracity and hypocrisy of Broadway has
always been evident—till now. And when a play which, like it or not
as you will, is serious, literate, individual in style, ablaze with talent,
and written without concern for Broadway values (it was originally intended for off-Broadway); when such a play is presented with taste
and economy, without abdicating to the star-system, the theatre-party
system, the fancy-advertising system; when the combined talents of a
remarkable cast working together in a way Broadway casts rarely do
serve to lift the work to "success" over the normal run of machine-
made mediocrities which reign supreme in our commercial theatre,
it seems to me cause for rejoicing rather than wailing and gnashing of
teeth. After all, there might be a better chance for a play more to the
Editor's personal tastes getting on the boards next time because
Virginia Woolf has at least shown it possible to draw a sizeable audience
without lowering its standards. Certainly, those Broadway wiseacres
who thought it didn't stand a chance are now revising their opinion of
what does.

It is possible, as the Editor says, that *Who's Afraid of Virginia
Woolf?* is "bad theatre, bad literature, bad taste"; it is also at least
equally possible that it is good theatre, good literature, good taste. Only
time will tell. In the meantime, I'm not asking the Editor to love my
girl as much as I do—that's what makes horseracing and marriages,
not to mention theatre criticism—but I do resent his directly labeling
her a degenerate whore. I believe the day will come when, as with that
other over-avid executioner, John de Stogumber, he will regret being
so quick to rush her to the stake.

Reality Is Not Enough: An Interview
with Alan Schneider

by Richard Schechner

SCHNEIDER: . . . If you're asking me to compare Beckett, Brecht, Pinter, and Albee: Beckett is Mozart—a string quartet—and Brecht becomes somebody like Stravinsky, where everything is going in all directions in some kaleidoscopic manner—highly romantic, or maybe that's the wrong word, in the sense of a sprawling, seeming disorder, but very rigidly controlled by his thematic material. It's like a great big bunch of varicolored scarves that you throw around, instead of one very small embroidered handkerchief—I don't think that's too profound an image. Pinter has been called a disciple, or at least a follower, of Beckett, and I think Pinter couldn't have existed as a playwright had he not read Beckett. But then he goes into his own field—a rhythmical, contrapuntal use of language and repetition of words, playing on words so that his plays are colloquial in a funny way and formal in another way— making some mystical thing out of the absolutely ordinary. Albee builds with words and emotions, too. Albee is highly theatrical—in *Zoo Story* he depends on a certain flair and sensationalism. (Sensationalism in *King Lear* is not bad either—it depends on what the sensationalism is about and whether it relates to the material.) I've often tried to analyze why I respond to these guys—is there a common denominator? I can't say that there isn't, but there doesn't have to be one, simply because I am lucky enough to direct their plays. I directed the Albee because he saw me do *Krapp's Last Tape*. I would have wanted to do Albee. I did immediately when I first read *Zoo Story*, which already had another director.

"Reality Is Not Enough: An Interview with Alan Schneider" by Richard Schechner. From *Tulane Drama Review*, IX, iii (1965), 143–150. Copyright © 1965 by *Tulane Drama Review*. Reprinted by permission of *The Drama Review*. The pages reprinted here form part of a longer interview.

SCHECHNER: Which was the first Albee that you did—*American Dream?*

SCHNEIDER: Yes. But I think it's dangerous to look simply for the similar elements—they're obviously similar in that they're all writers existing in the same contemporary universe. You notice what I have written up here: "There is no excellent beauty that hath not some strangeness in its proportion." That's Francis Bacon, the old one, not the painter. I think somewhere I must be attracted not just to the off-beat, but to the grotesque or the bizarre or the fanciful rather than the literal.

SCHECHNER: I want to talk about *Virginia Woolf*—about putting the production together. You worked with George Grizzard and Melinda Dillon at the Arena. Had you worked with Uta Hagen at all?

SCHNEIDER: I have known Uta slightly for many years—I went to school with her at the University of Wisconsin. I didn't know her well then, but over the years I've felt from afar a great respect for her work, and a great liking for her personally. She was everyone's first choice for the role from the moment we read it.

SCHECHNER: How long have you worked with George?

SCHNEIDER: George I've known since he was in high school. In his first appearance, he "crawled on" in a production I did of *Lute Song* at Catholic University in 1944.

SCHECHNER: How many productions had you worked with him before *Virginia Woolf?*

SCHNEIDER: About twenty, I'd say.

SCHECHNER: Melinda came out of Goodman, didn't she?

SCHNEIDER: Yes. I found her at Goodman and thought she was tremendously talented. She played Sonya in *Uncle Vanya* for me, and I thought she was incredible. I wanted her for the next year at Arena, because all she needed was experience. She auditioned for Zelda [Fichandler] but Zelda wouldn't hire her. So I said "I don't care if she's auditioning well or badly; you'll just have to take my word for it." Finally I really pressured Zelda, and of course, once she'd hired Melinda and watched her play in three productions, Zelda fell as much in love with her as we all did.

SCHECHNER: In how many productions had you directed her?

SCHNEIDER: Five or six.

SCHECHNER: And Arthur Hill—had you had any contact with him?

SCHNEIDER: I had seen him three or four times, and had written down in a little book "use this guy." He did not occur to us immediately as a choice for George. We had great difficulty, actually, finding a George, especially since the "powers that be" wanted to protect the "non-star" status of Uta with a star. But when we were rejected by the star we finally agreed to, Henry Fonda, somebody brought Arthur's name up, and we all jumped on it (except Edward, who didn't know him but took our word).

SCHECHNER: He did a magnificent job—much better than Henry Fonda would have done.

SCHNEIDER: No question about it. But again you have the thing I mentioned with Leontovich and Lindfors—two different styles of acting. Uta is Stanislavski; Arthur is what you might call the external school. And yet the reality he imparts in his way is as fine as Uta's. That's a great lesson, I hope, to everybody.

SCHECHNER: For all my objection to the play, I thought the acting was absolutely magnificent.

SCHNEIDER: There was one great advantage we had, apart from the luck in casting—that is, we got the right actors for all four roles—but, on top of that, we were sort of united against the universe. Also, there were only four, and they were almost always on stage. It was a concerted effort so, in a sense, the lack of time and the lack of having worked together previously was made up for by being all together, even offstage and outside rehearsal hours. We always looked forward to the four o'clock break, when we didn't just stop and have tea, but we'd stop and tell dirty jokes to each other, which was a way of cementing our relationship and getting rid of the tension. It was a tough show to work on—it was about the toughest show to stage that I've ever done—but it was also one of the happiest and most rewarding times I've ever had in rehearsal. Usually, Broadway rehearsals are just one agony after another.

SCHECHNER: I would like to, in as much detail as you can or will, go through the rehearsal of that.

SCHNEIDER: I had some idea when I read it of the texture that it had to have—it was not a literal view of life in 1964 on a particular campus; it was some kind of witches' sabbath.

SCHECHNER: How come you settled for such a real set?

SCHNEIDER: I can't say I settled or didn't settle; it was what the author wanted, and the first time around, the author should get what he wants. I think it could be done equally well with a very abstract set, but I understand why he wanted it. That set isn't so real. It seems real, and it's literal, but it's not real. It has all kinds of angles and planes that you wouldn't ordinarily have, and strong distortions. Edward wanted the image of a womb or a cave, some confinement. We've done it on the road with an open set, and it's pretty good, too. I think there's nothing wrong with having a room that's a hole they had to stay within. We always thought of the texture of the play as being simply intensified "reality"—the English critics said this was a Strindberg play rewritten by James Thurber, and those were the images we used. We certainly never thought of it as being realistic.

SCHECHNER: Can you take me through the rehearsals?

SCHNEIDER: I'll try. We read the play for three days because we didn't have Arthur, and Uta had eight million questions—some of which I answered, some of which Edward answered, some of which none of us answered. We changed some lines around, did some cuts. Then Arthur came, and we read the play for a couple more days while he asked questions. We tried to get a basic tempo, a basic texture, just vocally, so that the lines would be easier. Edward was terribly concerned with tempo—the beats, the basic rhythm of a scene. Uta wanted to get it on its feet as soon as possible; in this way she was following my strongest inclination, because I normally want to stage things fairly rapidly.

SCHECHNER: With the script in hand?

SCHNEIDER: It depends. I haven't for years said, "You've got to learn the third act by Friday." I used to, but usually they learn the third act when they feel like it. I wanted it staged as fast as I could, but I had a terrible time trying to plan the staging ahead of time. Usually I know the key scenes, but here I couldn't do even those; there were too many imponderables. So we worked on the staging, and it's a long play. We did it in about nine days, working fairly fast and fairly freely, basically working out what the logical relationships would be in the staging. It was about the hardest work I've ever done, because there was no indication of it in the script, and where or how they talked was not clear.

SCHECHNER: Did you block it, or, with a small cast, did they block it with you?

SCHNEIDER: They blocked it with me; I never just block a show, except in the cases like "Clov goes up the ladder."

SCHECHNER: You don't prepare a book for it beforehand?

SCHNEIDER: I normally do for the key scenes—I have some idea, but I try not to let anybody know I have the idea. But in this, I couldn't do it—I tried, I gave up. We worked it out very cooperatively and very little was changed.

SCHECHNER: What I'm driving at also is that an actress like Uta, with her Stanislavski training . . .

SCHNEIDER: I gave her a great deal of leeway. But Uta—and I must make this clear—was very pragmatic about the whole thing, Stanislavski or not. She'd say, "Look, shall I cross here because I've been over by the sofa too long"—she's very good at that, and I appreciated it. Once we'd answered the basic questions that had bothered her about motivation and meanings and relationships—Uta came prepared much more than I did; she had a notebook with a floorpan of the part of the room we didn't see.

SCHECHNER: How did you blend them all together?

SCHNEIDER: I don't know how to answer that. The point is, I don't remember where I gave in to Uta and where Uta was willing to try something. It was such an exhausting process from day to day that I didn't even make notes, mental or physical. All I know is the only major area where we had a problem was the "our son" business in the third act, which I don't think we succeeded in solving. I don't blame Uta; I blame myself for not being able to help her solve it. I'd like to see the third act solved better. Edward was blamed, but I don't think it was his fault as much as ours.

SCHECHNER: I'm driving for the technical, tiny bits of craft which define a director's style—of specific things you did.

SCHNEIDER: Well, that's hard to pin down. For example: everyone thought the opening scene of the second act with the two men was too long and should have been cut. I thought of it as a kind of chess game—all the scenes between them were chess games in which the two men who had contempt for each other would win a pawn, and we actually structured the scene around winning pawns. In their first scene, George says, "What made you decide to be a teacher?" and Nick says, "Oh, the same things that motivated you, I imagine," and he thinks he's off the hook. Then George says, "What were they?" and Nick says "Pardon?" "What were they?" repeats George, and Nick can only say, "I don't know." He's lost a point. Then George says, "You just finished saying that the things that motivated you were the same things that motivated me." He thinks he's got Nick pinned down, but the kid says, "I said I *imagined* they were." He slips out of it, a minor victory, but skillful skirting around the edge of conflict. So now he's won a pawn. That was the way we approached the whole thing. There's a kind of parry and thrust on a very subtle level, but each one's aware of it. Similarly, we built the second act scene of drunkenness on the sofa in terms of the two men. It's harder for me to talk about Uta and Arthur although, in effect, we worked the same way.

SCHECHNER: This is such an exhausting play for the actors . . .

SCHNEIDER: It's exhausting in one way and invigorating in another. Uta always said that when she played it right, she was never tired— not as tired as when she didn't play it right.

SCHECHNER: Did the life of the play ever carry offstage?

SCHNEIDER: No, I don't think so. I think this is an affectation that, honestly, I don't go along with. Uta was always backstage playing solitaire or kidding around, and she'd hear a cue and go onstage, and have a tremendous capacity for picking up the scene.

SCHECHNER: In terms of the over-all conception of the play, you said you saw it as a phantasmagoria. Do you have anything to add?

SCHNEIDER: It's also, in a funny way, very formal, very musical in structure, with rhythmical repetitions of elements and themes to be more stressed and less stressed, growing and fluctuating in intensity. I find it hard to go beyond that because, again, concept and execution rarely jibe. I started by saying that directing was an exploration. I felt this with *Virginia Woolf*—and I'm not talking about the success of the play or the audience reception, but what the production wound up as. Once we had those four actors, and once I had some sense of Edward's intention and his concern for formal structure— it was a symphonic score—we just had to be a little more intense here, a little simpler there.

SCHECHNER: Was there an over-all formal structure that you could find in it?

SCHNEIDER: Yes, I believe so, whatever symphonic form means. He'd given each act a title. The big problem was how to change the tone of the play halfway through; how to have a first act that could contain the third act, in essence.

SCHECHNER: Did you think you solved that?

SCHNEIDER: Partially. I tried to do it with the whole Berlin story, which I felt was terribly important. We didn't solve it completely; you never solve anything completely.

SCHECHNER: You've directed *American Dream, Virginia Woolf,* a revival of *Zoo Story,* and *Ballad of the Sad Café.* What do you think Albee's importance is?

SCHNEIDER: His importance is that he speaks and feels for the American moment that is *now,* and he's a talent that has only started. We haven't begun to see Edward's potential. His talent is not only in his personal statement, but when he can get outside it and be more objective—when he applies his emotional wallop and his use of language to more objective material, he'll be even more tremendous. Like in *Tiny Alice,* which I've just read. That makes *Virginia Woolf* seem like *Little Red Riding Hood.* . . .

Who's Afraid of Virginia Woolf?

by Harold Clurman

Edward Albee's *Who's Afraid of Virginia Woolf?* is packed with talent. Its significance extends beyond the moment. In its faults as well as in its merits it deserves our close attention.

It has four characters: two couples. There is hardly a plot, little so-called "action," but it moves—or rather whirls—on its own special axis. At first it seems to be a play about marital relations; as it proceeds one realizes that it aims to encompass much more. The author wants to "tell all," to say everything.

The middle-aged wife, Martha, torments her somewhat younger husband because he has failed to live up to her expectations. Her father, whom she worships, is president of a small college. Her husband might have become the head of the history department and ultimately perhaps her father's heir. But husband George is a non-conformist. He has gone no further than associate professor, which makes him a flop. She demeans him in every possible way. George hits back, and the play is structured on this mutually sadistic basis. The first cause of their conflict is the man's "business" (or career) failure.

Because they are both attracted to what may be vibrant in each other, theirs is a love-hate dance of death which they enact in typical American fashion by fun and games swamped in a sauce of strong drink. They bubble and fester with poisonous quips.

The first time we meet them they are about to entertain a new biology instructor who, at twenty-eight, has just been introduced to the academic rat race. The new instructor is a rather ordinary fellow with a forever effaced wife. We learn that he married her for her money and because of what turned out to be "hysterical pregnancy." The truth is that she is afraid of bearing a child though she wants one.

"Who's Afraid of Virginia Woolf?" From Harold Clurman, *The Naked Image: Observations on the Modern Theatre* (New York: Macmillan Publishing Co., Inc., 1966), pp. 18–21. Copyright © 1962, 1966 by Harold Clurman. Reprinted by permission of the publisher.

Her husband treats her with conventional regard (a sort of reflexive tenderness) while he contemplates widespread adultery for gratification and advancement in college circles. George scorns his young colleague for being "functional" in his behavior, his ambition, his attitudes.

So it goes: we are in the midst of inanity, jokes and insidious mayhem. Martha rationalizes her cruelty to George on the ground that he masochistically enjoys her beatings.

Everyone is fundamentally impotent, despite persistent "sexualizing." The younger wife is constantly throwing up through gutless fear. Her light-headedness is a flight from reality. The older couple has invented a son because of an unaccountable sterility. They quarrel over the nature of the imaginary son because each pictures him as a foil against the other. There is also a hint that as a boy George at different times accidentally killed both his father and mother. Is this so? Illusion is real; "reality" may only be symbolic—either a wish or a specter of anxiety. It does not matter: these people, the author implies, represent our environment; indeed, they may even represent Western civilization!

The inferno is made very funny. The audience at any rate laughs long and loud—partly because the writing is sharp with surprise, partly because an element of recognition is involved: in laughter it hides from itself while obliquely acknowledging its resemblance to the couples on the stage. When the play turns earnestly savage or pathetic the audience feels either shattered or embarrassed—shattered because it can no longer evade the play's expression of the audience's afflictions, sins and guilts; embarrassed because there is something in the play—particularly toward the end—that is unbelievable, soft without cause. At its best, the play is comedy.

Albee is prodigiously shrewd and skillful. His dialogue is superbly virile and pliant; is also *sounds*. It is not "realistic" dialogue but a highly literate and full-bodied distillation of common American speech. Still better, Albee knows how to keep his audience almost continuously interested (despite the play's inordinate length). He can also ring changes on his theme, so that the play rarely seems static. Albee is a master craftsman.

Strangely enough, though there is no question of his sincerity, it is Albee's skill which at this point most troubles me. It is as if his already practiced hand had learned too soon to make an artful package of venom. For the overriding passion of the play is venomous. There is no reason why anger should not be dramatized. I do not object to Albee's being "morbid," for as the conspicuously healthy William James once said, "morbid-mindedness ranges over a wider scale of experience than healthy-mindedness." What I do object to in his play is that its disease has become something of a brilliant formula, as slick and automatic as a happy entertainment for the trade. The right to pessimism has to be earned within the artistic terms one sets up; the pessimism and rage of *Who's Afraid of Virginia Woolf?* are immature. Immaturity coupled with a commanding deftness is dangerous.

What justifies this criticism? The characters have no life (or texture) apart from the immediate virulence of their confined action or speech. George is intended to represent the humanist principle in the play. But what does he concretely want? What traits, aside from his cursing the life he leads, does he have? Almost none. Martha and George, we are told, love each other after all. How? That she cannot bear being loved is a psychological aside in the play, but how is her love for anything, except for her "father fixation" and some sexual dependence on George, actually embodied? What interests—even petty—do they have or share? Vividly as each personage is drawn, they all nevertheless remain flat—caricatures rather than people. Each stroke of dazzling color is superimposed on another, but no further substance accumulates. We do not actually identify with anyone except editorially. Even the nonnaturalistic figures of Beckett's plays have more extension and therefore more stature and meaning. The characters in Albee's *The Zoo Story* and *Bessie Smith* are more particularized.

If we see Albee, as I do, as an emerging artist, young in the sense of a seriously prolonged career, the play marks an auspicious beginning and, despite its success, not an end. In our depleted theatre it has real importance because Albee desperately wishes to cry out—manifest—his life. The end of his play—which seeks to introduce "hope" by suggesting that if his people should rid themselves of illusion (more exactly, falsity) they might achieve ripeness—is unconvincing in view of what has preceded it. Still, this ending is a gesture, one that indicates Albee's will to break through the agonizing narrowness of the play's compass.

Albee knows all he needs to know about play-making; he has still to learn something other than rejection and more than tearfulness. His play should be seen by everyone interested in our world at home, for as Albee's George says, "I can admire things I don't admire."

The production—under Alan Schneider's painstaking direction—

is excellent, as is the cast. Uta Hagen, with her robust and sensuously potent *élan*, her fierce will to expression and histrionic facility, gives as Martha her most vital performance since her appearance as Blanche in *A Streetcar Named Desire*. She is an actress who should always be before us. George Grizzard is perfect in conveying the normal amusements and jitters of the mediocre man. Melinda Dillon as his debilitated spouse is appallingly as well as hilariously effective, and though I have some difficulty in accepting Arthur Hill, in the role of Martha's husband, as a tortured and malicious personality he does very well with a taxing part.

A final note: though I believe the play to be a minor work within the prospect of Albee's further development, it must for some time occupy a major position in our scene. It will therefore be done many times in different productions in many places, including Europe. Though I do not know how it is to be effected, I feel that a less naturalistic production might be envisaged. *Who's Afraid of Virginia Woolf?* verges on a certain expressionism, and a production with a touch of that sort of poetry, something not so furiously insistent on the "honesty" of the materials, might give the play some of the qualities I feel it now lacks; it might alleviate the impression of, in the author's pithy phrase, "an ugly talent."

The Riddle of Albee's
Who's Afraid of Virginia Woolf?

by Diana Trilling

. . . on the face of it, such a collocation of persons and events, or non-events, is unlikely material from which to fashion an appealing popular drama. Except for Martha and Nick's attempted sexual union, nothing has happened in Mr. Albee's play as we usually look for things to happen in plays: no one's life has been externally altered, everything that has taken place has been internal, precipitated by talk. Nor, as I say, is the "problem" of *Virginia Woolf* readily isolable in the quite extraordinary quantity of conversation indulged in by its four characters. Does the point of Mr. Albee's play lie in the overwhelming defeat and frustration of his characters, as it demonstrates itself in their most intimate connection with one another? Or is its primary concern the confusion which people like these make between reality and phantasy? Or perhaps these two themes merge and Mr. Albee is saying that where reality and phantasy are not kept distinct from each other, the result can only be despair and frustration? This, of course, would make an interesting proposition; but I am not sure it is Mr. Albee's, since a quite contrary case could be made for a reading of the play in which what Mr. Albee is saying is that reality, the modern reality, is too difficult to bear and that we must necessarily have recourse to self-deception—also an interesting proposition. At any rate, Mr. Albee's purpose in presenting us with these particular individuals caught in these particular dilemmas is pretty thoroughly ambiguous.

Then there are the characters themselves, so callous and undisciplined and violently vocal, so impartially destructive of themselves and each other. Who are these people, this history professor and his wife, who in their anguish go to such extremes of cruelty that they are robbed of all dignity and rob us of our dignity if we identify with them? Who are this monstrous young biology professor and his idiot wife who let themselves be held captive through such a long night of horrors and who even conspire in the unprecedented assaults of their hosts? After living in a university community through most of my mature life, I find myself strangely unprepared for the college Mr. Albee describes, or its faculty; and while I have a sufficiently elaborate imagination to suppose that many wonderful and awful things go on even in my own academic vicinity of which I am kept in ignorance, I'm still moved to comment on Mr. Albee's scene like the Victorian lady at the performance of *Macbeth*: "So different from the home life of our own dear Queen!" Indeed, the only shock of recognition I experienced in either seeing or reading *Virginia Woolf* was produced by its humor. The wit of Martha and George is not only familiar to me. My ability to appreciate its accuracy made me feel cozy and privileged—and I use the word "privileged" deliberately, for reasons I'll return to presently.

Now, to reserve judgment on Mr. Albee's play because its characters happen to be alien to one's own experience, because they are not representative, is surely to expose oneself to the charge of a peculiarly old-fashioned and even vulgar limitation of the imagination, since we all of us know that the purpose of art is to enlarge upon (which might mean exaggerate and distort) life, and that modern art is precisely defined by its refusal to be representational. Yet we keep it in mind that nothing in the technique or in the stylistic manner of *Virginia Woolf* is anything *except* representational. However brilliantly Mr. Albee maneuvers on a stage—and he operates with tremendous flourish —he is not writing in the mode of, say, Pinter's *The Dumbwaiter*, where it is at once established that the author's terms are metaphoric and that neither the situations nor characters are to be taken on the level of simple recognizable experience. Far more than Mr. Albee's play associates itself, at least in technical method, with the work of his more experimental contemporaries, it suggests comparison with a traditionally conceived play like Eugene O'Neill's *Long Day's Journey into Night*, to whose cast of sorely afflicted characters—a romantic actor and his drug-addicted wife; the actor's tubercular or alcoholic sons—the visitor from the university brings notably less preparation than to Mr. Albee's world. My experience of O'Neill's play—and I think it is one of the great plays of modern times—was nevertheless an experience of the momentous psychological and moral reality with which its author was able to endow his creations, a reality which quite transcends the merely familiar or recognizable. Even where a work is frankly representational in its method, in other words, the test of familiarity is in no sense final. The communication of reality is not dependent upon anything so simple as one viewer's personal acquaintance with the human or social material which is being represented. It is a matter of whether or not a recognizable truth is being spoken. For me, Mr. Albee's characters did not speak a recognizable human truth.

And, in fact, Mr. Albee's play was so far from confirming or altering my awareness of human reality that the idea came to me, leaving the theater, that perhaps in *Virginia Woolf* Mr. Albee had borrowed the terms of representation in order to write an allegory—not without ingenuity I decided that it was not a play about people but about the atomic bomb. The college, we recall, is called New Carthage. George is a professor of history, and that figures: history has failed, the work of the professor of history has been rendered meaningless by events. Martha is the humane tradition, or maybe just plain humanity, older than history, desperate in its reliance upon a failing historical destiny. Nick is the new man, as George regularly refers to him; he is science in cold command of himself and of the fate of mankind but impotent in his connection with humanity. His mindless wife, Honey, is the daughter of a dead religious faith which shored up the resources on which science now feeds while it goes about its grim task of destroying civilization. In this scheme of things, the childlessness of Mr. Albee's two couples would have sharp meaning: for us who live in the atomic age, the future may indeed be a phantasy. The only trouble with this reading of *Virginia Woolf* is that it is mine, not its author's. Mr. Albee has never given us any such account of his play. Nor does he need to; his play has made its way without allegorical exegesis: its audiences have no need for a variant reading; they understand Mr. Albee's play and accept it in just the terms in which it is offered to them, as a portrait of life as it actually is. For the American theater-going public, for the decent respectable middle-class people who night after night contemplate Mr. Albee's canvas of hopelessness and desperation, *Who's Afraid of Virginia Woolf?* is not only a good show. It is a good show which is also truth—moral truth, psychological truth, social truth, one or all of these truths, but truth.

Now it seems to me that if we are to know what we are about in our contemporary culture, it is of some importance to try to name this truth which Mr. Albee would seem so successfully to be communicating to his public, and to examine it to see just how truthful it really is. It is an enterprise which, far more than it asks a closer study of Mr. Albee's own assumptions in his play, demands an investigation of the culture, and in particular the literary culture, in which Mr. Albee has his existence as an author of high repute. For the point is that if Mr. Albee's public accepts his play as a true portrait of our contemporary state of being, this is not because of his skill alone, however skillful a playwright he indeed may be, or because he is able to enforce upon his audiences a view of life which, although only his, is yet able by some miracle of proselytization to prevail over the view his public brings with it to the theater. Mr. Albee's theatrical gift is manifest, as is his passion of conviction. But his literary culture is stronger than either his gift or his passion, and it has now been a considerable period of time that it has been the business of literature to teach us the defeat of life and to impress upon us the incapacity which we share with characters such as Mr. Albee's to rise above our awful destiny. Here, in fact, is the looming paradox of our contemporary culture, that while in our political life and in public affairs the liberal optimism which rests in a belief in the perfectibility of men and institutions is what sustains our efforts and guides our decisions, in our art this faith has for long years been conspicuously absent. The advanced art not only of our present decade but of this whole century, if it is to be understood at all, can be understood only as a refusal of all our liberal optimisms, as a negation of all of our liberal political and social hopes.

The conduct of the characters in Mr. Albee's play may be newly extreme, as the conventional theater deals with character. But there is nothing new to modern literature in the dark view of the human fate which Mr. Albee's people propose. When Mr. Albee tells us that his Martha and George are wretched beings or when he places alongside them his younger couple, Nick and Honey, in whom the wildness of a preceding generation has been replaced by the wedding of Nick's cold imperviousness with the noxiousness of a Honey, there is little in the writing of our time to refute his implied assumption that, from one generation to the next, humanity is caught in a grievous process of deterioration. Not only has our training in modern literature prepared us for just this vision of our human dilemma; it has carried us to the stage where we no longer think to ask for an alternative to people like these, or for an explanation of their woeful condition. The very absence of a feasible explanation of how people like Martha

and George, or Nick and Honey, came to be as they are makes, indeed,
the essence of the modern social indictment, in which things are shown
to be so inevitably bad that there is no longer any use in searching out
the social or personal causalities. If the people in Mr. Albee's play
suffer so strenuously, it is because this is conceived, not alone by Mr.
Albee but by the whole of our advanced culture, to be the only possible
outcome of modern life. The world being as desperate and ugly as it
is, people are desperate and ugly too. In our life of art, the evils of
civilization need no longer be specified.

In other words, to argue Mr. Albee's representation of the human
fate is to stand against more than one author of one play. It is to oppose the whole tendency of our artistic times. To voice any doubt on
the score of the familiarity or reality of the characters in *Virginia
Woolf* is to question what the literature of our day has made familiar
and insisted is real.

But to the inglorious determinism in which the advanced writing
of this period is rooted, to the conviction that suffering and degradation are now a destiny against which it is useless to struggle, Mr.
Albee would seem to have added another belief which has not yet permeated contemporary writing, or which, at least, is not yet a necessary
corollary of the deterministic position. This is the belief that although
we are forced by the grimness of modern civilization to live in defeat,
we make bad things worse by lying to ourselves and fleeing to the
solace of phantasy. Questioned about the meaning of his play, it was
indeed this aspect of it on which Mr. Albee put his own emphasis; the
New York *Times* quotes him as replying: " '*Who's Afraid of Virginia
Woolf?*' means 'Who's Afraid of the Big, Bad Wolf?' means 'Who's
afraid of living life without false illusions?' " A statement of this kind,
which suggests that we read Mr. Albee's play as an appeal on behalf of
reality, is bound to be arresting. And it may even mitigate our sense
that *Virginia Woolf* found its impulse elsewhere than in a recognizable
world—until we examine the reality which Mr. Albee's play opposes to
the life of false illusion and discover that it is always and only a
desert waste, so that if we strip his characters of what has been supplied
by illusion nothing is left but irremediable pain. Nor is this a tragic
reality that Mr. Albee counters to phantasy, since tragedy implies a
conflict between opposing forces—good against evil, free will against
determinism—and were we to throw off the bondage of our dreams as
Mr. Albee asks that we do, it could not possibly be to make a better
fate for ourselves but only to accept our defeat. Apparently what is

wrong with self-deception for Mr. Albee is not that it robs us of the strength to struggle in our own best interests but that it provides life with a meaning it doesn't have. It gives life content, and this, in Mr. Albee's view and in the view of most of the advanced writers of our time, is a priori a falsification; life has no content.

In short, the "message" of Mr. Albee's play couldn't be more terrible: life is nothing, and we must have the courage to face our emptiness without fear. Yet his play is a spectacular success. Day after day, week after week, a public made up of ordinary good, serious, hardworking, ambitious people well-enough situated in society to afford the considerable cost of a night at the theater, people who may not now be religious but who have religion somewhere not too far back in their tradition and who are still as much motivated by idealism as by cynicism, enjoy it and even feel grateful for it and personally confirmed by it. Why? The reason is worth groping for—but obviously I can only grope for it, I can only guess and share my guess.

A first, although superficial, explanation of the appeal of Mr. Albee's play would be that we all of us, however orderly the shape of our lives and whatever the idealism that still informs our moral systems, bring with us to the theater some sense of betrayal by, or at least disappointment in, our fates; Mr. Albee's grim view of the world, while it confirms us in this sense of victimization, also alleviates the guilt we have been taught to feel for our conspiracy in the defeats we suffer. We live in a period of acute uneasiness in which there has been added to our generalized and impersonal insecurity the special misery of holding ourselves accountable for the bad state of public affairs. W. H. Auden called a volume of his poems *The Age of Anxiety*. He could as well have called it the age of guilt or of self-distrust and pity, for these are all kindred emotions; that which we fear we also blame ourselves for having brought into being. Between, on the one hand, anxiety because of the frightening world we inhabit and, on the other hand, self-castigation because this is the kind of world we have created, the self-respect in which we base our idealistic values often has a hard time sustaining itself. Especially in our private lives, where recent psychiatry and sociology have taught us to look for the analogue and even the source of our public failures, our doubt of ourselves is likely to have its way with us unless we are given the confidence that our angers and frustrations, our bitterness and despair are not as egregious as we think them, that we aren't really as destructive as we accuse our-

selves of being, that there are others in worse case than we are, more
violent and undisciplined, sicker in heart and spirit. We go to Mr.
Albee's play and spend three hours in the company of people whose
disturbance is extreme. What might otherwise seem our perilous hold
upon ourselves has suddenly the look of a quite enviable self-control.
And we not only can forgive ourselves for our relatively inconse-
quential defections from the state of grace we ideally propose for ourselves. We also have Mr. Albee's word for it that where we do transgress
we have nothing of which to be ashamed: it is not our fault. The bad
condition, personal no less than social, of modern man is an inevita-
bility; it is his destiny, for which no cause need be named. Ugliness and
emptiness are the way things are and are bound to be.

Of course, judged in this light, Mr. Albee's play might be said to
constitute an exorcism. And this almost makes it art—until we note
how cheaply we have bought our relief and how comfortably we have
achieved our purge, certainly without either real pity or real terror.
The quality of the public response to *Virginia Woolf* need not be com-
pared to that which we give to the classic statements of tragic literature; we measure it against the response to (again) O'Neill's *Long Day's
Journey* and we recognize the significant difference between a pallia-
tive and a purgation. Of the performance of O'Neill's drama which I
witnessed I can say that I have never seen an audience at a modern
play so profoundly shaken by the truth with which it had been confronted. For here was a play about people who cared very deeply about
each other and who tried hard to be decent, people whose hopes were
right for themselves and each other, but who yet, for reasons beyond
their control because they truly reside in the human situation, had
defeated their decency, their love and hope. No one is shaken by Mr.
Albee's play. At most they are disquieted, which is a different order of
emotion. Indeed, what the majority of its admirers seem to take from
Virginia Woolf is not even disquiet but a quite opposite emotion,
reassurance—the perhaps embarrassed comfort we experience when
evidence is given us that we are not alone in what we had thought to
be misconduct and therefore need not judge ourselves harshly.

The bearing which such an emotion has upon our common childhood experience in the sexual sphere should be obvious. But no less
obvious, it seemes to me, is the part played in this dispensation of
solace by the superior station of Mr. Albee's characters, the fact that
the men are college professors and that one of the wives is even the
daughter of a college president. In classic tragedy, the heroes and

heroines with whose fate we are asked to identify ourselves are invariably of high station. By borrowing their nobility we are ourselves ennobled. In the advanced literature of our own day, the heroes and heroines, if we can call them that, with whom we make our identification are people who have been notably robbed of nobility. In contemplating their desperation we are meant to recognize our own despair. In remarkable fashion, Mr. Albee's play straddles these two conventions, and as a result reaches a much wider audience than has been so far appealed to by a writer like, say, Genet, whose characters are drawn from the underworld. Indeed, at the heart of any explanation of the success of *Virginia Woolf,* there lies, I think, this choice Mr. Albee has made, to place his drama in a university setting. Were his George and Nick, his Martha and Honey, a pair of suburban businessmen and their wives, it is highly improbable his play would have achieved its popularity. For it is not merely that *Virginia Woolf* depends on the superior articulacy of its characters as a substitute for action. Nor is it even that its ability to bring reassurance to its spectators derives from the fact that it speaks in the name of a class which is considered to have some moral as well as intellectual advantage over the rest of the population. More important still, the privileged position of Mr. Albee's characters permits his audience to identify itself with a supposedly superior class in our society, at the same time that it discovers the manifest weaknesses of this purportedly superior group.

We examine, for instance, the shock-value which *Virginia Woolf* can boast because of the overtness of its sexual content. Although contemporary writing has accustomed us to what would once have been an inconceivable boldness of sexual expression, this explicitness has up to now been largely associated with the conduct of persons of low or no class, chiefly classless bohemians. But Mr. Albee's bohemians are far from socially dispossessed; they may find no security in the class of their origin or in the status inherent in their professional choice but they do not disavow their station. We know exactly where they fit into the American class structure, loose as that may be. The obscenities of *Virginia Woolf* are spoken by people of the highest education who are free to move into our most valued and respected posts, and what could be more delightful to a general public than the discovery that this class which is supposed to have our traditional idealism in its keeping is itself anything but ideal? If even a college professor, trained in the best that has been thought and said throughout the history of civilization, can rage and storm like Mr. Albee's George, drink too much and

be so bewildered and lost, surely this is unimpeachable authority for
the rest of mankind which has not had his advantages.

In other words, the easy comfort that the public takes from *Virginia
Woolf* instead of the terror it took from Eugene O'Neill's play is associated with something more than moral and emotional reassurance,
important as these undoubtedly are. Together with forgiveness, Mr.
Albee's play provides another and even more subtle beneficence: it
offers its viewers a boost in the social climb, which, in present-day
America, means the cultural climb. In the very act of exposing our
cultural aristocracy as no better and indeed as even worse than the
rest of our society it confers upon its public the right to make this
kind of judgment in its own favor, a judgment to which there naturally
adheres a much-improved self-image.

I spoke of the "privilege" I felt because I was familiar with Mr.
Albee's humor. What I meant by this was that I was aware of a certain
cozy sense of cultural superiority because I was "in" on Mr. Albee's
idiom; the cultural experience which erased the distance which might
otherwise have interfered with a quick response to Mr. Albee's wit
represented to me a notable advantage I had over other members of
the audience to whom Mr. Albee's humor might perhaps not be so immediately available. It is just some such gift of advantage that I
think *Virginia Woolf* bestows on everyone who enjoys it, of being in
on the secrets of one's supposed cultural betters and of participating in
their supposed superiority even while disclaiming it. It is my belief, in
fact, that what finally accounts for the enormous popularity of Mr.
Albee's play is the unusual degree to which it fulfills a need which
more and more comes to govern our culture—the need for satisfaction
in our endemic quest for advantage, for privilege. . . .

The Ballad of the Sad Café

by Michael E. Rutenberg

The first of the three Albee adaptations is *The Ballad of the Sad Café,* based on Carson McCullers' novella of the same name. The play opened October 30, 1963, at the Martin Beck Theater to mixed reviews. Henry Hewes said: "This faithful, intelligent, and sensitive adaptation is the most fascinating and evocative piece of work by an American playwright . . . this season." [1] Martin Gottfried, however, called *Ballad* "a play of little theatre value." [2]

Notwithstanding the usual diversity of criticism a new Albee play engenders, most reviewers admitted that it was faithful to the novella with amazingly few changes in the story line. Notably, that the fight takes place out-of-doors instead of inside the café, and that the events of Amelia's short marriage to Marvin are not revealed to the viewer until somewhat later in the play than in the novella. To keep as close to the original prose as possible, Albee incorporated a narrator who, with minimal alterations, spoke the novella's lyrical passages. Originally, the playwright planned to use a tape recording of Carson McCullers speaking those passages, but the idea was dropped in favor of a narrator-stage manager as in *Our Town.* [3]

Much of the negative reaction to *Ballad* centered about Albee's decision to use a stage narrator. Most critics felt that his presence was alienating as well as undramatic. Walter Kerr in particular emphasized that the novella's material, use of chorus, and incorporation of a narrator, all conspired to cause alienation. [4] In a later article he returned to the same point and said, "in the theatre we should not need

"The Ballad of the Sad Café" (editor's title). From Michael E. Rutenberg, *Edward Albee: Playwright in Protest* (New York: Drama Book Specialists/Publishers, 1969). Copyright © 1969 by Michael E. Rutenberg. Reprinted by permission of the publisher and the author. The pages reprinted here form part of a longer chapter.

1 *Saturday Review,* Nov. 16, 1963.

2 Martin Gottfried, *A Theatre Divided: The Postwar American Stage* (Boston: Little, Brown and Co., 1967), p. 265.

3 *New York Herald Tribune,* Sept. 30, 1963.

4 *New York Times,* Oct. 31, 1963.

hired guides." [5] Robert Brustein was even less diplomatic when he described the narrator as having only one function: "to provide the information which the author has been too lazy to dramatize." [6]

While I don't hold to the belief that use of narration always constitutes undramatic playwrighting (we have only to look at Brecht), certain problems do arise from Albee's decision to use a narrator. Perhaps the most penetrating of these is the lack of motivation for the man to tell his story. As Albee has written it, we sense no impelling reason to listen to this grotesque love ballad. John McClain made a similar observation when he noted: "We don't, in fact, know very much about anybody in 'The Sad Café,' including the man who wanders through the proceedings, giving us only hints and suggestions." [7]

Miss McCullers clarifies the story for her reader early in the book by telling him what to expect. Albee, however, waits until page one hundred and sixteen before making the same point:

> *The Narrator.* The time has come to speak about love. Now consider three people who were subject to that condition. Miss Amelia, Cousin Lymon, and Marvin Macy . . . Now, the beloved can also be of any description: the most outlandish people can be the stimulus for love. Yes, and the lover may see this as clearly as anyone else—but that does not affect the evolution of his love one whit. . . .

Thus we have had to watch most of this adaptation with no intermission, without knowing why the narrator has chosen to submit us to this unpleasant tale of freakish love. We feel dislocated from the material and unable to focus in on the play. Robert Brustein corroborated this reaction when he wrote: "Because of my unfamiliarity with dwarf-loving lesbians, [the play] was rather lost on me." [8] *Newsweek* too, wanted to "know why they behave as they do." [9] It is my contention that had Albee kept to the chronology of the novella, and not tried to build suspense by holding off thematic material until very near the end of the play, the critics would have reacted more favorably to the play's grotesqueness.

Still another reason for the narrator's inability to pull his audience into the play stems from a sociological condition less prevalent in the

5 *New York Herald Tribune,* Nov. 17, 1963.

6 Robert Brustein, *Seasons of Discontent* (New York: Simon and Schuster, 1958–1965), p. 157.

7 *New York Journal American,* Nov. 10, 1963.

8 *Brustein,* loc. cit.

9 *Newsweek,* Nov. 11, 1963.

theatre today than when *Ballad* was first produced. As unflattering as
it is to our sense of supposed sophistication, as little as five years ago
the Broadway audience found it difficult to accept a Negro's omnip-
otence over the lives of white Southerners. They sat silent, feeling
that Albee intended a sociological comment, which of course he did
not.

The logical choice, it would seem, would have been to use Marvin's
brother, Henry Macy, as the storyteller. Henry has a special interest in
Amelia's story because it is his brother she marries. Having him step
into the play and out of it, as character-narrator (much like *Our Town*)
would have helped tie the two areas of the play together. Critic
Whitney Bolton saw the connection between Wilder's stage manager
and Albee's narrator:

> The function is all but identical . . . to describe the town, a building
> or buildings, the people, what happens in the town, how it came about,
> the state of the weather, to make commentary on events past and
> present. . . .[10]

Albee's narrator begins the play with an opening monologue that
serves to describe the off-stage town as well as introduce Amelia to us,
silently sitting at the window of her now boarded-up cafe. He takes us
back eight years in time and begins the play's events:

> *The Narrator.* . . . We are going back in time now, back even before
> the opening of the café, for there are two stories to be told: How the
> café came into being . . . for there was not always a café . . . and how
> the café . . . died. How we came to . . . silence.

The stage lights suggest evening, the boarded-up house once again becomes a general store, and with the entrance of some townspeople, the
dialogue begins.

Most of the talk centers about Miss Amelia's predilection for boot-
legging liquor and initiating lawsuits. The only other piece of gossip
we hear is that Henry Macy's brother, Marvin, is in the penitentiary.
Amelia then enters, her large frame looking quite masculine in Levis
and cotton work shirt. Hardly a page of conversation passes, when
along the dusty road comes a hunchbacked dwarf, suitcase in hand.
The dwarf declares he is "kin" to Miss Amelia and begs for shelter,
offering a fuzzy photograph of his mother and half-sister as evidence
that he and Amelia are, in some unexplained way, related. Never look-

10 *Morning Telegraph,* Nov. 6, 1963.

ing at the picture, Amelia contradicts her public personality and invites the little stranger in. He is not seen again for three days and
rumor has it that she has murdered the ragged dwarf for whatever it
was he carried in his suitcase. On the third night, determined to know
what has happened to the hunchback, the townspeople congregate at
Amelia's store. Just as they are about to confront her over the dwarf's
disappearance, the little man makes a startlingly grand entrance:

> COUSIN LYMON descends the stairs, slowly one at a time—imperi-
> ously, like a great hostess. HE is no longer ragged; HE is clean; HE
> wears his little coat, but neat and mended, a red and black checkered
> shirt, knee breeches, black stockings, shoes laced up over the ankles,
> and a great lime green shawl, with fringe, which almost touches the
> ground. The effect is somehow regal . . . or papal. . . .

The dwarf's kingly bearing and mended clothes completely baffle
the spectators into silence—broken only when the dwarf uncovers
Amelia's treasured snuff-box and partakes of its contents. Eventually
Lymon, whose name bears a striking resemblance to lemon and lime,
confesses that the powder in the box is only sugar and cocoa because
"the very teeth in my head have always tasted sour to me." The snuff-
box, or rather the possession of it, anticipates Lymon's eventual reign
over Amelia. It becomes his scepter, symbolically sweetening his life
with power, and the barrel he is perched upon turns into his throne as
he arrogantly holds court, interrogating his subjects. Two questions
emerge as significant. Stumpy MacPhail is first asked if he's married and
then if his wife is fat. Lymon apparently seeks to know what men are
available, showing his hostility if he finds that a man is married. This
sequence suggests Lymon's covert homosexuality which appears later
in the play as he unabashedly reveals his love and adulation for
Marvin Macy. Even at this early juncture Albee describes him as "like
a great hostess." Later clues to his womanliness will be discussed as we
encounter them in the story sequence. Cousin Lymon's presence has
undoubtedly changed Amelia's rather gruff disposition, for she now
allows liquor to be drunk on the premises and even encourages it by
giving out free crackers. Thus the transition from store to café is
accomplished.

Four years pass and the café prospers, during which time Amelia
and Lymon live together. The exact nature of their relationship is
never fully clarified, but it appears to be asexual, again underscoring
Lymon's latent homosexuality. During this interim Amelia appears

happier than she's ever been, despite Lymon's growing petulance. Only when love is mentioned does she revert to her old self:

> Cousin Lymon. (*Quite coldly*) Oh, Amelia, I do love you so.
> Miss Amelia. (*With some awkward gesture, kicking the dirt off a boot maybe*) Humf! Those are words I don't wanna hear. (*Pause*) Understand?

The relationship between this giant-woman (according to McCullers she should stand six foot two) and her homunculus companion, later complicated by Marvin's return from the penitentiary, is explained by Albee and McCullers in a rather superficial way, part of which has already been quoted:

> The Narrator. Now, the beloved can also be of any description; the most outlandish people can be the stimulus for love. . . . Therefore, the quality and value of any love is determined solely by the lover himself. . . .

This rather vague rationale for the dynamics of this twisted triangle does not suffice for what the *Times* referred to as a relationship "perverse enough to qualify as a psychiatric case history." [11]

The asexuality of the Amelia-Lymon relationship, however, does not alter the possibility of connubial symbolism. Specifically Cousin Lymon finds a tiny velvet box hidden away by Amelia and demands to know what it contains. The box, he is informed, contains two small kidney stones which Amelia had removed years ago. Having grown within her and caused great pain at their removal, the little mementoes become the children Amelia and Lymon will never have. He asks for them as a present, and when Amelia agrees to his request, she symbolically gives him his progeny without betraying his burgeoning homosexuality.

Another interesting bit of symbolism concerns the little acorn Lymon pilfers from Amelia's curio cabinet. The cabinet, like the café, represents Amelia's soul—gratuitously opened whenever Lymon wants entrance. The acorn, picked the day her father died and kept all these years, is a wish to remain as little as the seed because "little" is the childhood endearment her father would always use to offset her large size. But the acorn, not having fulfilled its natural function, remains undeveloped, reminding Lymon of his dwarfishness. Once his curiosity is satisfied he refuses Amelia's offer to have it.

[11] *New York Times*, Nov. 10, 1963.

As the play progresses, Lymon begins to become bored with Amelia, though she continues to try and entice him through extravagantly prepared meals. Professing no appetite, he nevertheless manages to finish what's given him—but not without assuring Amelia that he eats the fancy foods only as a favor to her. Lymon's refusal to return the love given to him by Amelia is exactly the relationship she prefers. She doesn't want her love reciprocated because then she must become responsible for someone else's emotional needs. Albee, faithful to McCullers' words, offers an explanation via the narrator:

> Therefore, the quality and value of any love is determined solely by the lover himself. It is for this reason that most of us would rather love than be loved; and the curt truth is that, in a deep secret way, the state of being beloved is intolerable to many; for the lover craves any possible relation with the beloved, even if this experience can cause them both only pain.

Amelia's story soon takes a new turn as Lymon learns of her short-lived marriage to Marvin Macy. Lymon forces Amelia to talk about "the most important fact of all in your whole life." Amelia's reluctant description of Marvin leaves the little man trembling with anticipation for the day they'll meet. Marvin soon becomes the very person whose masculinity will entice and encourage Lymon's personal fantasies. He loves the roustabout before he sees him because this hellion has the strength, the height, and the virility that Lymon can never attain. The attraction is ironically narcissistic because Marvin is really Lymon's dream of himself. There is also another aspect of Lymon's almost uncontrollable attraction to Marvin. Not having grown up with one father, Lymon continually looks for a father-substitute who will fill the emotional void this lack created. When Marvin facetiously suggests he adopt the hunchbacked dwarf, Lymon is ecstatic:

> *Marvin Macy.* You been followin' me around near a week now, wigglin' your ears at me, flappin' around, dancin' . . . you don't go home 'cept for your eats an' bed. What you expectin' me to do . . . *adopt* you?
>
> *Cousin Lymon. (With exaggerated longing)* Oh, Marvin Macy . . . *would* you? Would you do that?

Cousin Lymon's homosexual predisposition is not as far-fetched as some critics would have us believe. Albee has already shown in several places that the midget behaves and flirts like a woman—not that effeminacy is necessarily indicative of homosexuality. There are other more substantial clues to Lymon's hidden pathological orientation. Certainly he harbors a deep-seated resentment toward his mother and hence women in general, because it was in a woman's body that he grew stunted and misshapen. Once born, he watched his mother take on two more husbands after leaving his own father. By the third husband, Lymon, too, packed his little satchel and went in search of more stable "kin." Ironically, Lymon must destroy the very person who has sheltered him because in her maternal manner, Amelia is too reminiscent of his mother. Even his opening line in the play, "Evening. I am hunting for Miss Amelia," suggests that she will be his prey.

Psychiatrist Lawrence J. Hatterer in listing some of the many underlying causes of homosexuality has included the "inability and failure to relate to women because of hostility, [or] . . . as a means of obtaining the absent or ideal father . . . , or to fulfill the need to identify with a strong male through possession of that male sexually." [12] He adds that "the core of the homosexual's attraction and choice is narcissistic." [13]

Lymon wants to know why Amelia hasn't told him about the marriage and Amelia's only answer is: "He run off; he run off years ago; I ain't married to him no more!" What Amelia doesn't tell Lymon is that Marvin ran off at the point of a gun. Why she married the ex-thief and rumored rapist in the first place, and then never consummated the marriage, is not directly explained in either the novella or the play. Even Albee was curious enough to ask Miss McCullers, only to receive a shrug and with it the enigmatic answer: "That is what she would do." [14]

Yet, after reading both the novella and the play, enough facets of her personality emerge to explain her behavior adequately. Unfortunately, the answers are not clear in the play alone, and the reader must go back to the novella for clarification. Nevertheless, we can gather from information in both works that Amelia obviously married Marvin because she wanted a husband. What she didn't bargain for was Marvin's natural inclination for sex. Her fear of having children, because her own mother died in childbirth, would not allow her to take the chance that family history would repeat itself. Marvin's incontinence panicked Amelia and she finally had to drive him from

[12] Lawrence J. Hatterer, M.D., *The Artist in Society: Problems and Treatment of the Creative Personality* (New York: Grove Press, Inc., 1965), p. 139.
[13] *Ibid.*
[14] Personal Interview, March 17, 1965.

her or face her sexual phobia. Replacing Marvin with Lymon gave Amelia the opportunity to be the subservient wife without the threat of coitus. This asexual arrangement is perfectly acceptable to Lymon because his seeming conquest of Amelia gives him stature (she is taller than most men) without disturbing his homosexual orientation. In addition, Amelia could not reconcile herself to a life with Marvin because she bears too much resentment toward her father for being indirectly responsible for her mother's death. The more virile and masculine a man is, the more she is reminded of what killed her mother. Still, Amelia needs an object upon which to bestow her pent-up love, and the most appropriate recipient is the hunchback, Lymon; he is more feminine than masculine and offers no sexual threat to Amelia. Albee periodically refers to him as "Stirring, shy and coy, almost like a young girl."

Though Marvin is first repulsed by this "brokeback," Lymon is not deterred. The stunted cripple is willing to enslave himself to this symbol of masculinity in return for the privilege of remaining in his company. Marvin, seeing a way to get into the café—which he considers half his—allows the dwarf to befriend him. It isn't long before Marvin's plan is put into action when Lymon invites him to the café as his personal guest. In an ironic twist, Lymon begins to serve Marvin as Amelia had earlier served the hunchback. Marvin returns to the café night after night, drinking without ever paying, as Amelia, almost resigned to her fate, says nothing. Within a short time, Lymon arranges for Marvin to move into the café, giving the ex-husband Amelia's father's bed. Afraid of losing the dwarf, Amelia acquiesces to the arrangement:

> *Cousin Lymon.* Amelia! (*She turns her sad attention to him*) Amelia, I
> think I told you Marvin is gonna live here with us.
> *Miss Amelia.* (*Surprisingly helpless before his tone*) But . . . but, Cousin
> Lymon . . .
> *Cousin Lymon.* (*Giving orders, but taking a childish pleasure in the power
> of it*) Marvin Macy will sleep in your Papa's big bed, an' we will move
> what you have referred to as my coffin—my tiny bed—into your room
> . . . an' you . . . (*He pauses here for full effect*) . . . an' you, Amelia
> . . . well, you can pull up a mattress, an' sleep by the stove down here.

Albee's decision to put Amelia on a mattress by the stove, relegated to the status of family pet, is too degrading for her to accept. Being thrown out of her room is harsh enough. In the novella, Carson McCullers has Amelia sleep on the parlor sofa which softens the humiliation a bit. Her willingness to accept the degradation of the Albee version, is not in keeping with the personality of the woman who is about to fight with Marvin over who is to control the café.

The thought of the fight sends Lymon into spasms of ecstasy because in his mind they are fighting over him. Lymon tells Marvin, while the big man greases his body in preparation for the fight, to "be real slippery so she can't get a good grip on you." The advice could easily mean that previously she had had a good grip on the ex-convict—enough to emasculate and humiliate him in front of the town. One interesting aspect of this rather disgusting fight is that Marvin is not capable of winning without Lymon's help. When it looks as if Amelia might win, Lymon jumps on her back and hangs on, choking her. It is enough to turn the tide, and Marvin regains his position, beating Amelia into unconsciousness. Symbolically, it is Lymon—because of Amelia's love for him—who effects Amelia's destruction. The narrator then sums up the play's final moments:

> The Narrator. (Tableau, with MARVIN MACY, COUSIN LYMON together, MISS AMELIA sprawled on the porch) Marvin Macy and Cousin Lymon left town that night, but before they went away, they did their best to wreck the store. They took what money there was in the café, and the few curios and pieces of jewelry Miss Amelia kept upstairs; and they carved vile words on the café tables. After they had done all these . . . they left town . . . together.

Deciding not to take over the café, the two men depart, never to be heard from again. Amelia, in a final moment strangely reminiscent of Lavinia in O'Neill's Morning Becomes Electra, retreats into the house to spend the rest of her life in despair and isolation.

What is perhaps the most surprising aspect of Ballad is its similarity to still another play: Sartre's No Exit[15] Both plays reveal the dynamics of unfulfilled love. In the Sartre play, three rather despicable people are placed together in one room. They have been picked by the powers in control (it seems they have died and are now residing in hell) to clash psychologically with one another until the room becomes hell to live in. What kind of human triangle produces psychological hell? Sartre puts a lesbian in with a whore who can't stomach her and seeks, instead, the solace of a man who is repulsed by her promiscuity and looks to the lesbian as a symbol of masculine triumph. Ballad

15 Jean-Paul Sartre, No Exit and Other Plays (New York: Vintage Books), pp. 1–47 [No publication date].

offers much the same situation. Amelia is in love with Lymon, who rejects her in favor of Marvin. Marvin is not interested in the dwarf except to use him as a means to getting at Amelia who continues to rebuff him. Walter Kerr noticed the sado-masochistic libidinal linking and analyzed the trio's interaction: "It is clear . . . that each of these figures is destroyed by the one he loves. . . ." [16] An interesting note to the comparison of the two plays is that Colleen Dewhurst was chosen for the part of Amelia after being seen in a television showing of Sartre's *No Exit,* where she played the lesbian.[17]

The Sartre play works because the group is put together as punishment for certain crimes committed against society. It doesn't make any difference how personally repugnant they are; we do not have to empathize with them in order to react positively to their retribution. *Ballad,* however, creates the same hellish situation (even to its constant reference to heat) when it should have created an environment filled with compassion. The proximity of the play's characters and situation repel us, where the novella's lyric distance intrigues us. *Newsweek*'s critic talked of basically the same thing when he commented that the play "is clothed in the too, too solid flesh of living actors, [making] these phantasmal beings lose the unreality that made them real." [18]

In the last analysis, the events of *Ballad* do not stand up to the intriguing concept that initiated the work; namely, that for some, the state of being loved is intolerable. What happens is that the theme becomes subverted by an overwhelming sense that what we see is not the human condition, but a freak show. It becomes impossible to identify with a petulant, vengeful dwarf, an ex-drug-pushing rapist, or a hostile, semi-ignorant, frigid woman.

Albee's ever-present concern with the outcasts of society has mistakenly led him to recreate for the stage what is, despite its haunting lyricism, essentially not engrossing dramaturgy.

16 *New York Herald Tribune,* Nov. 17, 1963.
17 *New York World-Telegram and Sun,* Oct. 29, 1963.
18 *Newsweek,* Nov. 11, 1966.

The *Tiny Alice* Caper

by Henry Hewes

Although the returns are far from in on Edward Albee's new play, *Tiny Alice,* post-opening discussions with its author, its director, and its two stars may be helpful to those who wish to ponder its mysteries.

As most theatergoers know by this time, *Tiny Alice* is the story of a cardinal's secretary whose soul is sold to the richest woman in the world (Miss Alice) in exchange for a huge annual contribution to the Church. However, there is such constant suggestion that each character and event symbolize larger and not fully comprehensible forces that many of us ask, "What does it all mean?" or complain that the story-telling has been exasperatingly interrupted by the endless embellishments.

The critical response has been amazingly contradictory. Some have used such phrases as "a masterpiece," "one of the capstones of the drama's long and adventurous history," "every minute a totally engrossing evening," and "establishes Albee as the most distinguished American playwright to date." Others have deprecated it with such terms as "prolix," "tedious," "pretentious," "ostentatious," "ugly," "wilfully obscure," "an intellectual shell game," "a set trap that has no bait." Dominating the reviews, however, are those that combine extravagant praise and condemnation. "Big and brutal as an Elizabethan tragedy" is followed by "more depraved than any drama yet produced on the American stage." "Falters badly at the beginning of the second act" is balanced with "the most engrossing evening of contemporary theater you are going to find in New York this year." Many reviewers have confessed a complete inability to find meaning in it at all, while others have discovered parallels to the Bible, to *Parsifal,* and to *Alice in Wonderland.*

There is also some difference of opinion among the production's principal participants, each of whom has avoided a direct interpretation of the play's meaning.

To begin with, Mr. Albee (pronounced *All*-bee) is fuzzy in his recollections about the play's origins. Like the play's protagonist, Julian, he is obviously no longer sure how much of his memory about its creation is real, and how much dreamed, imagined, or hallucinated. He says, "I think the play started a couple of years ago when I read a small news item about someone in Germany who had been kept in a room within a room." At the time he had been working on another new play, *The Substitute Speaker,* which he decided to postpone because it contained superficial resemblances to *Who's Afraid of Virginia Woolf?* The title *Tiny Alice* occurred to him some time later but was not consciously arrived at from any literary source such as *Alice in Wonderland,* any more than the protagonist's name, Julian, had any relation to an actual Julian such as the emperor who renounced Christianity for paganism, or the off-Broadway producer who recently martyred himself by going to jail.

Actually, the Miss Alice we see in the play is a woman pretending to be Miss Alice, who in turn is a necessary personification of the abstraction Tiny Alice. The latter figuratively lives inside the huge model of a house, in the living room of the same house in which the play takes place. One gathers from Mr. Albee, however, that these relationships were not planned but came about as he wrote the play. He points out, "For me the process of writing is the process of discovery. I began by learning to know my characters. To do this I keep testing them in my mind to see if I can say how they would react to situations they will *not* meet in the play. Then I try to pretend that these characters have their head, though perhaps there is an unwritten outline in my unconscious that pushes them one way instead of the other."

Just as Mr. Albee used the name Nick in *Who's Afraid of Virginia Woolf?* to suggest that the character was related to Nikita Khrushchev and was therefore an exponent of a totalitarian society, so he occasionally enriches moments in *Tiny Alice* with verbal puzzles. For instance, Julian will paraphrase the words of Jesus, but to interpret Julian as Jesus would be carrying the analogy further than the author intended. On a more realistic level, the playwright reminds us that most religious people relate themselves to Christ in their hallucinations. And he also believes that Julian is like many religiously dedicated people in being subconsciously motivated by sexual repression.

Sir John Gielgud, who plays Julian, has not discussed the play's mysteries with Albee. For him Julian is not Christ but a man who, like Christ, wanted to be a martyr. Furthermore, he feels that it is perfectly all right for him not to understand the meaning of the play, because Julian is written as an innocent who does not fully understand what is happening to him. Nevertheless, he has asked questions about the play's intention of the director, who could answer him in such a way as to protect his performance. Explains Sir John: "I find the cynical and rather superior attitude of the intellectual actor dangerous. Intellectually I didn't like *Endgame.* Yet if I'd played it I might have. In *The Lady's Not for Burning,* I felt I didn't understand a word of it, but somehow understanding its atmosphere was sufficient. The director should tell you just enough so that you won't have a disbelief in what you're doing. Disbelief can destroy a performance, but belief, even in tosh, can be effective."

Gielgud does not find *Tiny Alice* "tosh," but he admits having felt a tiny disappointment at the third act as it was when they went into rehearsal. While he now feels that the third act has been much improved and the second act possibly weakened by the revisions that have since been made, the end of the play still strikes him as negative, with a huge Alice coming through the door as he dies. (He prefers a discarded ending that would have left him tied to the model house with rope, facing a slower death.) Nevertheless, director Alan Schneider has urged him to play the present ending more ecstatically, as if Julian in his final moments had come to discover certain things. "It's not negative," insists Mr. Schneider. "Was the death of Christ negative?"

For two other reasons the ending may seem more negative than was intended. First of all, the sound of heartbeats and heavy breathing as the doors open have been widely misinterpreted as being those of an increasingly terrified Julian, whereas they are meant to belong to whatever comes through the door. Then, too, Mr. Albee admits that his original notion (since abandoned) had been that the ending would be played inside an attic closet and include a fifteen-minute monologue (as it will in the published version). "I think it might work in a film," he says, "but in that enormous living room you can't get enough close-up concentration to hold the audience, so we cut Julian's final speech down to five minues." While the author intended the ending to be terrifying, he also wished to leave the audience with two possibilities for Julian: total hallucination or the personification of the abstraction.

More satisfactory for Sir John is the seduction scene, which calls for the expression of sexual ecstasy and religious ecstasy at the same time. He says, "The two are very similar, but also very different. Onstage they must both be inner emotions. And since I have three ecstatic moments in the play, I must try to make each of them interesting and in some way different."

As his temptress partner, actress Irene Worth finds this boldly lusty scene less difficult than the one in which she prays that they shall not be consumed. "It's the most difficult thing I've ever done," she says. "It's so abstract, and I have to define it on three levels—the general fear of being consumed by fire, the specific fear of giving in to a part of my nature and falling in love with Julian, and the religious urge to rededicate myself to Alice."

Another difficulty for Miss Worth is establishing the fact that she is not Miss Alice, but merely an employee required to impersonate Miss Alice through endless escapades like this one. For this action is complicated by her emotional involvement when she finds herself in danger of falling in love with Julian, and this is why there is rage at her from above that sets fire to the house's chapel.

Miss Worth believes that the play urges us to stop using religion as armor to protect ourselves from the abstraction which is God (or Tiny Alice). Since the infinity of the universe cannot be defined or expressed, Julian has the choice of being a surrogate (remaining alive with Miss Alice), or "finding the center of the sun" (dying in the presence of Miss Alice), or going back to the asylum.

Whatever their variations of opinion on the meaning of *Tiny Alice*, all those interviewed are agreed on the quality of this play. Sir John feels that, like Fry and Eliot, Albee has tremendous feeling for rhythm and music and that the play has great beauty and ambitiousness of scale. Miss Worth likes it because the play is full of marvelous moments when it "strikes dead center and resounds in true overtones." And Alan Schneider calls it one of the two or three finest plays he has ever directed (he has directed, among others, *Waiting for Godot, The Glass Menagerie, The Skin of Our Teeth, The Collection, The Caucasian Chalk Circle,* and *Who's Afraid of Virginia Woolf?*).

If you pin Mr. Schneider down, he will tell you that *Tiny Alice* surpasses Albee's previous play because it digs more deeply into areas of truth and because its poetic and theatrical imagery is more sophisticated. He adds, "For example, Julian's confession about his hallucinations is more symphonic in structure and richer in language than the 'Bergin' speech in *Virginia Woolf*."

While at this stage of its run *Tiny Alice* is doing even better business than its predecessor, Mr. Schneider feels that the six daily critics have done the play a disservice with all their talk about its perplexity. "None of them got the point. I think this play is absolutely simply. It's a parable about man and the universe, about what we *choose* to do. Its point is expressed in the third act when Julian is told clearly what they want him to do and why. As a director my job was mainly to see that it was performed truthfully, and to find an exact blend of real and unreal that would suit the play."

While Mr. Albee thinks he has written a good play, he is aware of the possibility that he may have made some mistakes. He says, "I expected the audience to be able to become deeply concerned with Julian's predicament. If it cannot, something is wrong." He denies the allegation, however, that his play attacks the Church, insisting that he sees as evil only the uses to which people put things and the power structure. And he also denies that he tries to create "shocking" plays. He is seconded in this denial by Mr. Schneider, who argues that the use of such conventionally taboo words as "ejaculation" in the theater are infinitely less shocking than is, for instance, the distorted unnatural representation of life in the slick magazines."

Mr. Albee seems more hurt than angry when he explains, "I've never put anything in a play in order to shock the audience. I try to write only those things that *these* characters would say at *this* time. I don't concern myself with the audience's reaction. However, if people are taken out of their concentration on the action by shock it is unfortunate."

On the other hand, the playwright wishes the audience would come to *Tiny Alice* with fewer preconceptions, to experience the play as we experience music. "If you are not a trained musician," he says, "you intuit the structure of the piece by osmosis." Thus, as an author, he is most concerned with construction and with getting the play's musical rhythms right, and he is convinced that if he does this honestly and well, people will respond to the play even if they are confused about it or dislike what they think it says. "What matters is not whether the play coincides with how a critic thinks it should be written, or what a critic thinks of what it says," argues Mr. Albee. "What a critic should tell his reader is how effectively he thinks the play has said whatever it chooses to say."

As I closed my notebook, I wondered if Mr. Albee would have been pleased if someone had called *Tiny Alice* "a play that unfolds with great skill, whatever the hell it is choosing to say."

The Play That Dare Not Speak Its Name

by Philip Roth

In *Who's Afraid of Virginia Woolf?*, Edward Albee attempted to move beyond the narrowness of his personal interests by having his characters speculate from time to time upon the metaphysical and historical implications of their predicament. In *Tiny Alice*, the metaphysics, such as they are, appear to be Albee's deepest concern—and no doubt about it, he wants his concerns to seem deep. But this new play isn't about the problems of faith-and-doubt or appearance-and-reality, any more than *Virginia Woolf* was about "the Decline of the West"; mostly, when the characters in *Tiny Alice* suffer over epistomology, they are really suffering the consequences of human deceit, subterfuge, and hypocrisy. Albee sees in human nature very much what Maupassant did, only he wants to talk about it like Plato. In this way he not only distorts his observations, but subverts his own powers, for it is not the riddles of philosophy that bring his talent to life, but the ways of cruelty and humiliation. Like *Virginia Woolf*, *Tiny Alice* is about the triumph of a strong woman over a weak man.

The disaster of the play, however—its tediousness, its pretentiousness, its galling sophistication, its gratuitous and easy symbolizing, its ghastly pansy rhetoric and repartee—all of this can be traced to his own unwillingness or inability to put its real subject at the center of the action. An article on the theater page of *The New York Times* indicates that Albee is distressed by the search that has begun for the meaning of the play; the *Times* also reports that he is amused by it, as well. When they expect him to become miserable they don't say; soon, I would think. For despair, not archness, is usually what settles over a writer unable to invent characters and an action and a tone appropriate to his feelings and convictions. Why *Tiny Alice* is so unconvincing, so remote, so obviously a sham—so much the kind of play that makes you want to rise from your seat and shout, "Baloney"—is that its surface is an attempt to disguise the subject on the one hand, and to falsify its significance on the other. All that talk about illusion and reality may even be the compulsive chattering of a dramatist who at some level senses that he is trapped in a lie.

What we are supposed to be witnessing is the destruction of a lay brother, sent by the Cardinal to whom he is secretary, to take care of the "odds and ends" arising out of a donation to the Church of two billion dollars. The gift is to be made in hundred-million-dollar installments over a twenty-year period by a Miss Alice; the wealthiest woman in the world, she lives in a castle with her butler and her lawyer, each of whom has been her lover. On a table in the library of the castle stands a huge model of the castle itself; deep within the replica, we are eventually encouraged to believe, resides the goddess Alice, whose earthly emissary, or priestess, or cardinal, is the millionairess, Miss Alice. In the name of, for the sake of, Alice, Miss Alice sets out in her filmy gown to seduce Brother Julian; once that is accomplished, a wedding is arranged, presided over by the Cardinal. At this point Miss Alice promptly deserts Julian—leaving him to Alice, she says; the Cardinal turns his back on what he knows is coming and takes the first hundred million; and the lawyer shoots the bridegroom, who dies with his arms outstretched, moaning at the end, "I accept thee, Alice, for thou art come to me. God, Alice . . . I accept thy will."

None of this means anything because Albee does not make the invention whole or necessary. The play strings together incidents of no moral or intellectual consequence, and where the inconsistencies, oversights, and lapses occur, the playwright justifies them by chalking them up to the illusory nature of human existence. It is as though Shakespeare, having failed to settle in his own mind whether Desdemona did or did not sleep with Cassio—and consequently leaving the matter unsettled in the play—later explains his own failure of imagination by announcing to the press that we can never penetrate reality to get to the truth. The world of *Tiny Alice* is mysterious because Albee cannot get it to cohere. To begin with, the donation of two billion dollars to the Church is irrelevant to the story of Julian's destruction—what the money will *mean* to the Church doesn't enter his mind. In fact, though he is sent to the castle to make arrangements for the gift, not a word is said of the money until the Cardinal appears at the end to pick up the cash, and then we learn that Church lawyers have been working out the essentials of the deal on the side. And why does the

Cardinal want the money? Hold on to your hats. Though he dresses like a prince of the Lord, he is really greedy!

Least convincing of all is what should be the most convincing—Tiny Alice Herself, and the replica, or altar, in which her spirit resides. The implications of a Woman-God, her nature, her character, and her design, are never revealed; but is this because they are beyond human comprehension, or beyond the playwright's imagination? Though *his* God is mysterious, certainly the Cardinal could discuss Him with some conviction and intelligence (and ought to, of course, instead of appearing as a pompous operator). Why can't Miss Alice or the lawyer discuss theirs? Why don't they answer the questions that are put to them? There is, after all, a difference between the idea that life is a dream and a predilection to being dreamy about life. But withholding information is Albee's favorite means of mystifying the audience; the trouble comes from confusing a technique of dramaturgy, and a primitive one at that, with an insight into the nature of things.

> *Butler.* This place [the real castle] was in England.
> *Miss Alice.* Yes, it was! Every stone, marked and shipped.
> *Julian.* Oh, I had thought it was a replica.
> *Lawyer.* Oh no; that would have been too simple. Though it is a replica . . . in its way.
> *Julian.* Of?
> *Lawyer.* (*Points to model*) Of that. (*Julian laughs; the lawyer says*) Ah well.

But instead of getting him off the hook with "Ah well," why doesn't Albee press the lawyer a little? Why doesn't Julian inquire further? For a lay brother who is, as he so piously says, "deeply" interested in the reality of things, how little persistence there is in Julian's curiosity; how like a child he is in the answers he accepts to the most baffling mysteries that surround him. Indeed when Albee begins to see Julian as a man who walks around acting like a small boy in a huge house full of big bad grownups, he is able to put together two or three minutes of dialogue that is at least emotionally true. To the delights and dangers of the Oedipal triangle (boy in skirts, mother in negligee, father with pistol) Albee's imagination instantly quickens; but unfortunately by presenting Julian as a befuddled boy, he only further befuddles the audience about those metaphysical problems that are supposed to be so anguishing to Julian as a man. For instance, when a fire miraculously breaks out in the chapel of the castle and in the chapel of the replica, one would imagine that Julian, with his deep interest in reality, would see the matter somewhat further along than he does in this exchange:

> *Julian.* Miss Alice? Why, why did it happen that way—in both dimensions?
> *Miss Alice. (Her arms out)* Help me.
> *Julian.* Will you . . . tell me anything?
> *Miss Alice.* I don't know anything.
> *Julian.* But you were . . .
> *Miss Alice.* I don't *know* anything.
> *Julian.* Very well.

That is the last we hear of the fire. But how *did* it happen? And why? I know I am asking questions about the kind of magical moment that qualifies a play for the Howard Taubman Repertory Theater for Sheer Theater, but I would like to know who this Alice is that she can and will cause such miracles of nature. Might not Julian, a lay brother, who has the ear of a Cardinal, rush out to tell him of this strange occurrence? But then the Cardinal exists, really, only as another figure to betray and humiliate poor Julian, the baffled little boy. As a Cardinal, he is of no interest to Albee, who seems to have introduced the Catholic Church into the play so that he can have some of the men dressed up in gowns on the one hand, and indulge his cynicism on the other; he does nothing to bring into collision the recognizable world of the Church and its system of beliefs, with the world that is unfamiliar to both Julian and the audience, the world of Tiny Alice. Such a confrontation would, of course, have made it necessary to invent the mysteries of a Woman-God and the way of life that is a consequence of her existence and her power. But Albee is simply not capable of making this play into a work of philosophical or religious originality, and probably not too interested either. The movement of the play is not towards a confrontation of ideas; it is finally concerned with evoking a single emotion—pity for poor Julian. In the end the playwright likens him to Jesus Christ—and all because he has had to suffer the martyrdom of heterosexual love.

Tiny Alice is a homosexual day-dream in which the celibate male is tempted and seduced by the overpowering female, only to be betrayed by the male lover and murdered by the cruel law, or in this instance, cruel lawyer. It has as much to do with Christ's Passion as a little girl's dreaming about being a princess locked in a tower has to do with the fate of Mary Stuart. Unlike Genet, who dramatizes the fact of fantasying in *Our Lady of the Flowers,* Albee would lead us to believe that his fantasy has significance altogether removed from the dread or the desire which inspired it; consequently, the attitudes he takes towards his material are unfailingly inappropriate. His subject is emasculation—as was Strindberg's in *The Father,* a play I mention because its themes, treated openly and directly, and necessarily connected in the action, are the very ones that Albee has so vulgarized and sentimentalized in *Tiny Alice*: male weakness, female strength, and the limits of human knowledge. How long before a play is produced on Broadway in which the homosexual hero is presented as a homosexual, and not disguised as an *angst*-ridden priest, or an angry Negro, or an aging actress; or worst of all, Everyman?

A Psychiatrist Looks at *Tiny Alice*

by *Abraham N. Franzblau*

The psychoanalytic concept of the fierce, often fatal struggle in man between Eros, the life force, and Thanatos, the death drive, may help to throw some light on *Tiny Alice*. For the play's mood continuously reflects the psychoanalytical concept of ambivalence, and its techniques are a blend of theater and Freudian "dream-work," reality and fantasy, obliging us to apply to it not the logic of the intellect, which has failed all those limited to its spectrum, but the logic of the unconscious, that same logic that enables us professionally to unravel a dream or cure a crippling phobia.

From this vantage point, *Tiny Alice* is seen to examine a number of philosophical problems that have always puzzled man. What is reality? Is it the castle or the replica? Is the fire burning in the model or in the chapel itself? If the latter, why do we see smoke and flames? Are things the way they seem to our senses, or is there an ultra-reality or an ultra-perception? Are there eternal values which a man can cherish and to which he can anchor his life, or is it all "vanity of vanities"?

Albee's character delineation of Julian, the lay brother, goes from the almost smug equilibrium to which a lifetime of religious dedication has brought him, to the pitiful, hopeless clutching at the splinters of shattered dogma—in fact, of all of his values and ideals—as he lies dying. What is happening? Why? The wife turns away. The cardinal, whose secretary he was, turns away. The lights in the replica of the castle go out one by one. In a Kafkaesque scene, more like a nightmare than any play ending in the realm of reason, he slowly dies without knowing what he did to merit death or why he is left to die alone. None of his beliefs affords him any clue. The scene echoes Freud's queries about whether all religious dogma does not stem from man's unwillingness to accept mortality, to recognize the rapacious cruelty of nature, or to sacrifice some of his libidinous gratifications for the help he needs from his fellow men.

Does Albee offer any answers? He does not. He pinions the absurdities of life, its inequities and iniquities, focuses his microscope upon it, and leaves you to react. *Tiny Alice* forces you to question and to ponder. Albee tries to pluck the masks from life and death, sex, love and marriage, God, faith, and organized religion, money-greed, wealth, charity, and even celibacy. Part of our puzzlement undoubtedly comes from believing that some of these do not wear any mask, but are solid and authentic, at least in our personal value system. But no one comes out of the theater with all of his own psychological blinders and colored glasses still in place.

And therein lies the reason we are disturbed and puzzled at the same time as we are fascinated. Albee penetrates the superficial layers of our conscious personality and, using the mysterious escalators of the unconscious, reaches the citadels of our private certainties and shoots them full of question marks.

John Gielgud and Edward Albee
Talk About the Theater

by R. S. Stewart

Albee began: "Not being an actor, I would assume that an actor probably thinks about a part a much longer time than a playwright does. I would imagine that actors think about some parts twenty years before they even try to play them. Isn't that true, John?"

"To some extent," Gielgud said. "I was very lucky in playing most of the big parts I wanted to play when I was pretty young, and so I had to go at them without thinking too much about them beforehand. But Edith Evans said to me not long ago: 'I know just how I should say that last line of Queen Catherine'—that was in *Henry VIII,* which we did together about eight years back. When you're older you do look back on parts and you think, I could play Romeo, I could play Hamlet better now—though I would know better than to try. That was one of the reasons why I directed Burton's *Hamlet,* to be of some use through experience in helping a younger actor avoid some of the technical snags which you find in playing a part like Hamlet. With older parts like Lear or Prospero, which I would hope to play again someday, I put them right away from my mind and never think about them again until the time comes to do them.

"But with a play like yours I can hardly imagine putting it away and taking it up again in a few years. It was just a unique moment: you wanted me to play it, and I'm very happy to try. Of course I was very frightened of playing this part in *Tiny Alice,* and the first thing I wrote you, you remember, was 'how old do you think this man is?' And you tactfully wrote back and said, 'I think that all the people in the play are round about fifty,' which consoled me a little bit in my temerity of

"John Gielgud and Edward Albee Talk About the Theater" by R. S. Stewart. From *The Atlantic Monthly,* CCXV, iv (1965), 61–68. Copyright © 1965, by The Atlantic Monthly Company, Boston, Mass. Reprinted by permission.

being seduced and dying in two big scenes, for which I thought I had really passed the limit."

Albee interrupted with a slight qualification: "I don't know whether I thought that everybody in the play was to be fifty—it really never occurred to me when I was writing the play what ages the people were going to be. Style and content codetermine each other. The nature of the characters and how they speak and how old they are: all these things codetermine each other. Quite often in plays that I've written before, it seemed to me that a person would be of a certain age, but in this one it didn't seem to matter very much. There's no particular country; there's no specific locale nor any age given. The most important thing was to get the proper actors. I don't think that American actors, for the most part, have been trained sufficiently to do roles that are out of the realistic theater, but that was a secondary consideration, and in casting *Tiny Alice* my major concern was to get the actors who could do the roles the best."

"Naturally I am enormously flattered," Gielgud said. "None of the young English avant-garde playwrights has dreamt of writing me a part, and I've always had the feeling that because I was a bit skeptical about the 'kitchen sink' school in London that school rather despised me as being of the Establishment and a bit snooty, and that I didn't have any appreciation of the new theater that had come into being because it might rather push me out of the center of the stage—which is not true at all.

"It's a terribly ugly age; ugliness is made a fetish"

"The fact remains that I have longed for some years, while being very doubtful of my ability to understand and interpret the new playwrights, to have a shot at one of them because one longs to create a new part more than anything in the world and to find a challenge for one's experience by playing something completely different. But if I happen not to be in sympathy with the feeling of a play when I read it, I just can't like it. That has been the case with many of the avant-garde plays in England, though I've been an enthusiastic admirer of Harold Pinter since he began.

"As regards the standard of acting in America, I've not been able to see the companies at Stratford, Ontario, and Stratford, Connecticut, which have done such tremendous work with the classics the last few years. Of course since I've been here there's been all the trouble at the Lincoln Center, and it's odd, isn't it, that *Tiny Alice* should seem to need actors with classical training even though it is a very modern play. But it would appear that the two kinds of theater are more closely allied than one would think at first."

Albee nodded and then spoke: "I think there's a considerable relationship between what's referred to as the avant-garde play and the classical play. At the same time I've always insisted to people who find Samuel Beckett incomprehensible, for example, that I've always found his plays totally naturalistic, though they're not naturalistic in the sense that people usually understand the term, in the post-Chekhovian sense—"

"I've never been able to admire Beckett," Gielgud interrupted. "It's one of my completely blank spots. His plays are very difficult for me to take. I suppose I am used to climaxes and effective curtains and action and vivid and glamorous characters. To me it's very depressing to go to the theater and see completely gloomy and subhuman characters in despair, but I suppose this has something to do with the reaction after the last war and the feeling of the world being in a terrible state, worse than it's ever been in history before. I find that your play, Edward, on the other hand, has a kind of grandeur and a certain glamour which make it exciting to me in a way the Beckett plays that I've read and seen have not been."

Albee laughed: "Maybe *Tiny Alice* is *de*vant-garde and will set the theater back about forty years!"

Gielgud laughed with him: "Some people think that Zeffirelli has set the theater back fifty years, pictorally speaking, and yet his *Romeo and Juliet,* because it is directed to be acted in an earthy, naturalistic style, has been thought to be something absolutely modern and new. What is so fascinating in all art is that it always seems to be rebounding on itself, and the things that are new one minute turn out to be quite old-fashioned the next, and vice versa. And yet really what I suppose people of my age feel is that it's a terribly ugly age, that ugliness is made a fetish, ugliness and frankness and outspokenness, in a way that we were brought up to consider was in very bad taste. But who shall say what is bad taste from one moment to another?"

"I've always thought," Albee broke in, "that it was one of the responsibilities of playwrights to show people how they are and what their time is like in the hope that perhaps they'll change it."

"Well, I suppose that's true," Gielgud went on. "That's what's exciting about the theater—we're always remaking ourselves in terms of different people's imaginations and different people's experiences and the movement of the world, which is so tremendously quick now that one seems to *have* to rethink things. . . .

"I suppose I must enjoy playwriting," Albee said, "since I do it; I try not to do things that I don't enjoy. Being a playwright is enjoyable except for that six-week period from the first day of rehearsal until the day after opening, which is the worst time in the world. Writing in itself is exhilarating, absorbing, involving. I can't think of anything else that I'd rather do.

"I try to let the unconscious do as much work as possible"

"How does it happen? I usually discover that I have started thinking about an idea which I know is going to be a play. This process may take anywhere from six months to two and a half years, and during that period I don't think about the play very much except that I realize from time to time that I *have* been thinking about it, and when the characters who are going to be in the play begin to take shape, I improvise with them.

"I choose a situation that's not going to occur in the play itself and test the characters out to see how they behave in it, how they react within that situation, what they will say to each other in a situation of that sort. And when they start behaving on their own and take over from me and seem quite natural and believable in an improvised situation, then I suppose I know that it's time to start writing the play.

"I try to let the unconscious do as much work as possible, since I find that's the more efficient part of my mind. The actual writing itself usually takes a fairly short time—the shorter plays and the one-act plays anywhere from a week to three weeks. The two longer plays have taken about three weeks or a month an act. But it is enjoyable; it must be."

"I sort of smell a play," Gielgud said. "When I first read *The Lady's Not for Burning* by Christopher Fry, which was then as revolutionary in style as your play is now, I didn't understand it very well, but I fell in love with it, and I handed it across the railway carriage to the manager I was traveling with and said, 'I love this play; can we do it?' and he bought it for me. . . .

"The maddening thing to me is that an actor, unlike a playwright or any other artist, cannot destroy his work if he doesn't really think it's completely successful. Writers very often rewrite their plays without success, but at least they can abandon them unproduced. But actors have to give a performance, for better or for worse, before an audience, and be blamed for it if it isn't good, and therefore our unsuccessful experiments are far more damaging than in any other profession."

"I wonder if that's really true?" Albee asked. "Actors are very seldom blamed, at least in the United States, for the failure of a play. It always seems to be the author. But to go back to what I was saying before about writing a play: there are two interesting moments of discovery. The time of sitting down at the typewriter and finding out what you have been thinking about—that's rather exciting. Then, in spite of the anguish of it, the rehearsal period is exciting too, because then you find out to what extent what you had thought the play would look and sound like can relate to what emerges. And this really doesn't have much to do with acting or directing; it's how close your vision can be realized. It's quite fascinating. . . ."

Gielgud interrupted: "You know that Shaw once said that you should be able to write the entire plot of a good play on a postcard. I can't imagine that you could follow this advice with regard to your play now."

"Could you do that with *Hamlet,* for example?" Albee asked. "What is the plot of *Hamlet?*"

"Well, I don't know," Gielgud said. "I once tried to explain the plot of *Twelfth Night* to Debbie Reynolds, who was going to read two speeches in Hollywood for a picture, and I got into such terribly deep waters with Olivia and Viola, and which characters were disguised as ladies, and which were in love with gentlemen, that I really had to give up."

"Shaw should have known better than to say that," Albee added, "because sometimes he wrote prefaces half the length of a play not explaining even half the play."

"I think," Gielgud went on, "he only meant that the essential point of a play should be able to be expressed very easily and simply. But I rather agree with you. I don't think you can do it with Shakespeare, and I doubt if you can even do it with the Greeks."

"I shouldn't think so," Albee said. "I would think that if a play can be stated in a couple of sentences, that should be the length of the play. One writer was asked to explain one of his books and he took a copy down and started reading, and he said, 'I will stop when I get to the last page of the book, and that's what it's about.' I think possibly Shaw was joking, possibly kidding himself."

Gielgud laughed: "Besides, of course, he was very fond of writing postcards!"

"The pressure on playwrights to sell out to what
the audience wants is enormous"

"The theater's always been in a crisis," Gielgud said. "Everything that comes along—television, movies—we always say, 'No more theater, we've killed it.' The music hall—the variety stage, I mean—certainly had a crisis, which pretty well destroyed it. There's no more variety really; it's moved into other fields—movies and television. There's too much entertainment. Nowadays, too much entertainment is thrust on the public, whether they like it or not, so that they've become soporific and are apt to accept anything they're given. The writers have gone to Hollywood and to television, and there are not enough good writers to go round. Everything has to go much faster."

Albee disagreed: "Both in England and the United States there are quite enough playwrights. I suspect there are more young playwrights in the United States and England right now than there have been in the past thirty years put together. And in the United States and England there are quite enough fine actors and directors to handle the work of these good, exciting young playwrights. The basic crisis the theater's in now is that the audience primarily wants a reaffirmation of its values, wants to see the status quo, wants to be entertained rather than disturbed, wants to be comforted and really doesn't want any kind of adventure in the theater, at least from living playwrights— they'll take it from dead ones because that's part of lit-cult.

"The pressure on playwrights to sell out to what the audience wants is enormous. They don't have to go to Hollywood; they don't have to write for television; they're encouraged to sell out even if they stay in New York and write for the theater. Actors sell out in order to earn a living and to support their families; they're encouraged to play in bad plays because primarily it's the bad play that the audience wants. But there's no lack of good playwrights, no lack of good actors.

"One of the things that happened, in New York at any rate, was that the off-Broadway theater came into existence to fill the enormous gap. The result was that three or four years ago, I think, there were one hundred and twenty productions off Broadway, a lot of them by exciting young playwrights with all the actors working for absolutely next to nothing to fill the gap that existed on Broadway, where the important plays weren't being done."

"In a way, the same thing happened many years ago in England," Gielgud said. "When I was first in theater, in the early twenties, we did some Chekhov plays in a little tiny theater, which was a converted movie house across the river in Hammersmith. They were very successful, and we all played for ten pounds a week. These were the first interesting—and fashionable—successes of Chekhov in England, and at that time Chekhov was as advanced as you or Pinter is today.

"So there's always been this movement, and nearly always the young actors and the young playwrights have got their first chances for less money and have made their reputations from the ground floor, which is the right way. After all, every craftsman has to learn his trade, and I don't think there's any harm in young actors and young playwrights having a hard time at the beginning of their careers. It only spurs them on to do better."

"I agree that it's wonderful," Albee said, "that the young actors should get their training, as you say, on the ground floor and suffer a little bit.

> *"It's a very difficult thing to say where the*
> *commercial theater becomes cheap . . ."*

"But I think it's ironic and unfortunate that once they have gotten their training in excellent plays, they're encouraged to go on to the larger theaters and do plays that aren't so good."

"That's quite true," Gielgud said. "But how do you really classify a play that's not so good? What do you mean by a bad play?"

Albee smiled and then answered: "What I mean by a bad play is a play I don't like, naturally."

"Well, that's what I mean too," Gielgud said. "But it's a very difficult thing to say where the commercial theater becomes cheap, isn't it?"

"You can tell, I suppose, the *intention* of a work," Albee said. "You can tell by the intention if it's written for what the audience wants."

"I haven't seen it yet," Gielgud went on, "but *Luv* is obviously as good as *The Typists* and *The Tiger*, which were a great success off

Broadway. Now *Luv* is as big a success on Broadway, and I imagine it has exactly the same quality and first-class presentation, so there's nothing wrong with that, is there? Things are always relative. I think that the extraordinary thing is that we managed to keep going in both countries during the war and since the war, when everybody came back shaking to the core and everything was changed, values were changed in every direction."

"I don't really think it is relative," Albee said. "One season, I don't remember which one it was, the '59–'60 or the '61–'62, the following playwrights—and this is only a partial list—were not performed in the commercial theaters on Broadway: Beckett, Brecht, Genet, Ionesco, O'Casey, de Ghelderode, Shaw, Shakespeare, Strindberg, Ibsen, Chekhov —that's a partial list. These people weren't performed on Broadway; every one of them was performed off Broadway. Actually, I think off-Broadway shouldn't exist. All the plays done off Broadway should be done on Broadway. I think the commercial theater, appealing as it must be to a larger audience, does sin somewhat, and I do think that actors and directors and playwrights can be swept into this morass altogether too easily."

"Well, I'm grateful for the commercial plays I've acted in. I've played in plays by Coward and by N. C. Hunter and even by Priestley and Knoblock. They were all commercial plays; they were very successful. I enjoyed playing in them because they gave me a new public and I was able to develop new skill as a performer. I think an actor ought to know how to play 'boulevard' comedy as well as mystery plays or thrillers or farces. Nobody could say that Rex Harrison hasn't increased his status as a performer by his performance in *My Fair Lady,* which is one of the finest pieces of virtuoso acting I ever saw in my life. And he was equally brilliant, I understand—although unfortunately I didn't see it—in a play of Chekhov's called *Platonov,* I think, which he did at the Royal Court for only about four or five weeks.

"No one should dare to criticize an actor for being as skilled and as versatile as that. If he can decorate a very smart comedy by Roussin or Noel Coward brilliantly, then it justifies his appearing in it. I think that every actor has the right to do that, especially if he can vary it by playing the classics, and the experience will help him in playing in a modern play like yours."

"Indeed," Albee said. "But the point is that there should be competitive coexistence. I've no objections to the musicals and the sex comedies inhabiting our commercial theater. The objection I have is that they *inhibit* our commercial theater, and there's no competitive coexistence with the more important plays, or damn little."

"There will always be that kind of theater in any great capital city," Gielgud said. "There's no doubt about it, you won't get rid of it however much Brecht you push on. I don't think you will ever have a big commercial success with a Brecht play in any country except possibly in Germany. Certainly they haven't been either in England or here. I've always thought the cult of Brecht highly overpraised, personally, and I've never understood why everybody goes mad about him. I have read the plays in translation—I don't speak German—and I find them very unpalatable except for their purely theatrical quality. The wonderful way they were directed in Berlin was what appealed to me.

"It's the same thing with Peter Brook's *Marat Sade* play, which has been such a success in London. I couldn't take in the literary details of the play, but the theatrical presentation delighted and thrilled me. I suppose as an actor one is more inclined to be taken by that, and that's where one sometimes quarrels with authors who naturally want the written word to be the most important thing." . . .

"Is Tiny Alice *meant to be intentionally confusing?"*

"What can I say about *Tiny Alice*?" Albee asked himself. "The play is not supposed to be terribly easily apprehensible. It's meant to contain things that the audience must take out of the theater with them and think about.

"Now there have been some objections to this—the play is obscure and difficult. I can't understand this as being a complaint about a play. If a play is confused and muddled in its thinking, then that's bad writing. But if a play demands a little bit from the audience, including the audience of critics, then I don't think that's a failure on the play's part. Or am I getting defensive?"

"I read a notice," Gielgud said, "which claims that the audience coughs all through this play. Well, this is quite untrue, because I listen for the coughs like an eagle, and if there is a cough I've not a bad idea of how to stop it—at any rate, I have a jolly good try. The fact remains that this is a most holding play. I said at rehearsal, though you weren't present, that nobody would ever sit through my death scene—they'll all be charging out getting their snow boots. But I must say I haven't seen anybody leave before the end of the play.

"And this is the magic of the theater, which you never get in a movie quite in the same way because it's set forever, whereas the performances in a play can vary like the ticking of a metronome. We actors count on the audience as a sort of sounding board, and they count on us to give them the excitement and the stimulus which they come into a theater to get. If both sides give enough of it, then the result is usually an exciting and rewarding performance, and I think this play, from what I feel on the stage, supplies that excitement practically all the way through, which is a very rare thing, and this is really the test of an acted play.

"Oh, of course it's not an easy play. I think there are many things that are very confusing, but I think you meant that. I've often lost my way when I'm watching a play. I don't think seeing a play once you can ever take in all the details of it. Many people have told me they want to see it again. I'm sure countless people will want to read it."

"You're quite right," Albee agreed. "How can one possibly say one likes a play and not see it a second or a third time." He stopped and pondered for a moment: "Is *Tiny Alice* meant to be intentionally confusing? I wonder if I meant it to be intentionally confusing. Maybe I meant it to be something a little different from confusing—provocative, perhaps, rather than confusing."

Gielgud broke in: "From the ordinary standpoint it seems that there are a great many threads that you don't bother to tie up, but presumably you did this quite deliberately. They don't affect the way we act it, I don't think. It's a very rare thing to have a play, as you said earlier, in which there is no locale definite, in which the ages are not definite, in which the time of day is not particularly defined, and which still seems to have a wonderful suspense value. One wants to know what will happen to the characters in the next situation, and this is something you've contrived, I think, amazingly successfully.

"The actual content, the metaphysics, and the arguments do baffle me in quite a number of cases. Most of those places we discussed at rehearsal, and you modified some of them, changed some of them, cut others. I think there are still things which could be straightened out perhaps, but you've written the play and you've completed it, and presumably that's what you wanted to say."

"It's never what I've wanted to say," Albee said. "I always find things I want to change; but curiously, the only bafflement that you show in playing the part of Julian is the proper bafflement that Julian must feel."

"The wonderful relief," Gielgud said, "that I had about this part was that I was *supposed* to keep wondering what it was all about. I was on easier ground than the other actors, who are supposed to know what they're about."

Albee interrupted: "And the audience has got to follow the play through you because you're the innocent coming into this rather extraordinary assemblage of people."

"What is more difficult for the audience," Gielgud said, "is the relationship between the other people. I think that the relationship between the butler and the lawyer—in fact, the butler's whole position in the play does seem to me to be rather unexplained. Another thing that has always confused me is why you never let Julian refer to the 'deal.' He must know that he is the go-between with the cardinal and that the money has been offered through him. In fact, Miss Alice implies many times that the deal will fall through if Julian doesn't behave as she wants. But you've never allowed me specifically to refer to the money in any way. I suppose it's something to do with the innocence of my character, but I've always wondered—when I'm dying they take the money, and the cardinal leaves with it, and I never quite know whether to be even aware that this has happened.

"It is a point in the character that I rather fail to understand. Of course I'm diverted by her questioning in the first scene with Miss Alice; but throughout the entire play I never refer directly to the deal, to the matter at hand. It's only obliquely referred to."

"In the beginning, the innocence," Albee said. "In the end, because you're preoccupied with your own dying and not with who is carrying off what suitcase full of papers. And also because the whole arrangement about the money was more of a pretext. . . ."

"But in a way," Gielgud interrupted, "it is the fundamental point of the play. I'm not at all worried by the fact of *why* she wants to give her money away; I think that's a perfectly good premise to start the play on. I think that the more difficult things are when you begin to wonder whether it's Alice who is also directing the three protagonists —the woman, the lawyer, the butler—as well as presumably directing *my* steps to come to her, which is what she really wants and what they really want."

"We're sounding now as we did in the first week of rehearsal," Albee said. "And the play is already open. I guess we have to assume that that scene took place in the intermission between the first and second acts. There is one other thing, however, and it's going to sound like the proper thing to say, except you must believe I don't say the proper thing. It's that I can't imagine the play better acted or better directed. I say this only in gratitude and not as obligation." He suddenly smiled: "I know you want to know what the play is about, John, but I don't know yet, so I can't say."

Gielgud smiled and then broke into laughter: "I hope I shall know by the end of the run."

Tiny Alice

by C. W. E. Bigsby

The central idea for *Tiny Alice* came to Albee as he was reading
a newspaper account of a man who had been kept imprisoned inside
a room which was itself inside another room. Something about this
"Chinese-box" situation appealed to him both because of its relevance
to the problems of dramatic structure and because of the fascinating
metaphysical aspects which these contingent realities suggested.

When the play first appeared in New York, its reception was something less than ecstatic. At best it was thought to be a personal therapy
paralleled perhaps by Tennessee Williams' *Camino Real*; at worst it
was a confidence trick pulled on the world in general and the drama
critics in particular. When the dust had begun to settle and the play
was published, Albee's bland assurance, in an author's note, that the
meaning of the play was so clear as to obviate comment did little to
convince those who had been completely baffled by the performance
itself. Neither did it serve to redeem a work which unquestionably remains more effective in print than on the stage.

The play opens in a garden as a Cardinal and a lawyer discuss a
billion-dollar grant which Miss Alice, a young but apparently eccentric
semi-recluse, wishes to make to the Church. An implied condition of
this grant, it seems, is that the Cardinal's secretary, a lay-brother called
Julian, shall be sent to arrange the final details. In his eagerness to
concur, the Cardinal is obviously prepared if necessary, to sacrifice not
only his secretary, but also his dignity and principles.

When Julian goes to the castle in which Miss Alice lives, it becomes
apparent that she, in conjunction with the lawyer and her butler, is
part of a conspiracy aimed at seducing him away from the Church. But,
in the place of spiritual commitment, they offer him only reality, an

"*Tiny Alice.*" From C. W. E. Bigsby, *Albee* (Edinburgh: Oliver & Boyd, 1969). Copyright © 1969 by C. W. E. Bigsby. Reprinted by permission of Oliver & Boyd Ltd.
and the author. The pages reprinted here form part of a slightly longer chapter.

uncompromising and unattractive alternative to one who has sheltered behind expansive illusions. For the world with which they confront him is a restrictive place in which the individual is cut off from any final consolation and forced to create his own meaning and identity. Although Julian eventually marries Alice he refuses to accept the "tiny" world for which she is the surrogate. The conspirators are thus forced to shoot him and leave him to discover the truth of their precepts as he faces his death.

If the need to face reality was the main principle which emerged from *Who's Afraid of Virginia Woolf?*, then Albee had done little to define exactly what he meant by reality in that play. He had made no attempt to integrate the metaphysical world into his picture or to assess its validity as a part of the reality to which he urged his characters. With *Tiny Alice* he remedies this and attempts to analyse the whole question of religious faith.

Nevertheless, there is a direct connexion between *Tiny Alice* and *Who's Afraid of Virginia Woolf?*, between brother Julian's religious reveries and George and Martha's frenetic distractions. For when Albee stresses the relationship between spiritual ecstasy and erotic satisfaction, as he does by emphasising the sensuous nature of Julian's visions, he is not intent simply on making a cheap debating point about the nature of evangelical power. His thesis is rather that the individual craves a spiritual distraction just as he craves a carnal one—as a substitute for a frightening reality. Just as Nick had turned to sexuality as a retreat from the real world, so Julian turns to religion for much the same reason. Where George had created a fantasy son to fill a vacuum in his own life, Julian "creates" a son of God.

Indeed Albee is at pains to point out that Julian's early religious conversion had stemmed, not from a sudden sense of mystical enlightenment, but from fear. Afraid to face the implications of a world which seemed both empty and pointless, he had abdicated his responsibility by positing the existence of a god—a process which Albee elaborates in some detail. Julian describes the frightening situation of a person who finds himself locked inside an attic closet. In order to retain sanity that person is forced to assume the existence of somebody who can eventually open the door and release him. To Julian this is an apt description of his own "conversion," for, as he admits, "My faith and my sanity . . . are one and the same." [1] The need to personify this abstrac-

---

[1] *T.A.*, p. 45. [Edward Albee, *Tiny Alice* (New York, 1965)—Ed.]

tion leads logically enough to a belief in God. In another story/parable Julian describes the moment in his childhood when he had first felt the need to create this abstract "saviour." He explains that, after he had been severely injured in a fall, his calls for help had gone unanswered. Gradually his call had changed from an appeal to his grandfather to a plea to God, whose non-appearance is accountable, and who is the personification of the need to be helped. Thus for Julian the abstract world clearly represents an apparent compensation for the inadequacies of the temporal world and man's fear of loneliness. It is interesting to note just how closely this explanation of religious conversion matches that given by Alain Robbe-Grillet in an essay entitled "Nature, Humanism, Tragedy." He sees this process, though, as an arrogant extension of humanism by which the individual seeks to exaggerate his significance. While Albee would reject this particular interpretation, he nonetheless clearly shares his belief that this strategy represents an inauthentic response to life. "I call out. No one answers me. Instead of concluding that there is no one there . . . I decide to act as if someone were there, but a someone who, for one reason or another, refuses to answer. The silence that follows my outcry is hence no longer a true silence, it is now enhanced with content, with depth of meaning, with a soul—which sends me back at once to my own soul . . . my hope and my anguish then confer meaning on my life . . . My solitude . . . is transformed at last by my failing mind into a higher necessity, into a promise of redemption." [2] But, as Robbe-Grillet goes on to warn, if this is "a path towards a metaphysical 'beyond,' " it is also "a door closed against any realistic future;" for if "tragedy consoles us today, it also forbids all more solid conquests for tomorrow." [3]

For all Julian's desire to believe in an after-life which will grant some kind of retrospective meaning to the real world, he is unable to place his faith wholeheartedly in this man-made God. Indeed it is this element of doubt, the fact that he remains fundamentally "dedicated to the reality of things, rather than their appearance," [4] which at one stage had taken him to an asylum, his faith temporarily lost, and which makes him an ideal subject for the conspiracy. For the conspirators sense that he is "walking on the edge of an abyss, but is balancing. Can be pushed . . . over, back to the asylum/ . . . Or over . . . to the

2 Cited by Herbert Kohl, *The Age of Complexity* (New York 1965), p. 233.
3 *Op. cit.*, p. 234.
4 *T.A.*, p. 138.

Truth." [5] The truth with which they confront him is the need, in Alice's words, to "accept what's real." [6]

But this is precisely the crucial question: just what is "real?" Is reality simply the limited world of human possibilities in which death provides an apparent proof of futility, or is it the more expansive world in which "faith is knowledge" [7] and the individual an element in a grand design? Who is right, the existentialist or the determinist, the secularist or the Christian? Should Julian place his faith in God, "Predestination, fate . . . accident," [8] or should he embrace the restricted world of human suffering and love?

Distrusting language, as he had in *The Zoo Story* and *Who's Afraid of Virginia Woolf?*, Albee chooses to dramatise this dilemma in symbolic terms. The central symbol which he uses is that of a "model" castle which dominates most of the play. This "model" seems to be an exact replica of the castle within which the action takes place. It is accurate in every detail. When a fire breaks out in the larger castle it also breaks out in the "model." But Julian is uncertain in which of the two it had originated, and therefore uncertain as to which is the original and which the copy. This Platonic paradox clearly lies at the very heart of the play, as it does of Julian's crisis of conscience. For he remains unsure of the true nature of reality until the very end of the play, when he is converted, as Martin Buber would say, "to this world and this life." [9] In symbolic terms, this is represented by his acceptance of the "model" castle as the "real" one and the larger version as merely a projection of it—an interpretation which the lawyer himself endorses when he says of the castle in which he lives that "it *is* a replica . . . Of that . . . [*Pointing to the model*]." [10] The conspiracy, therefore, is evidently devoted to convincing Julian that he should accept this apparent diminution of his concept of reality. As the lawyer advises him, "Don't personify the abstraction, Julian, limit it, demean it." [11]

While Plato's idea of the real world clearly differed in kind from Albee's, one feels that they would both concur in Plato's belief that the

---

[5] *T A.*, p. 106.

[6] *T.A.*, p. 167.

[7] *T.A.*, p. 165.

[8] *T.A.*, p. 160.

[9] Rev. James Richmond, *Martin Buber* (Nottingham 1966), p. 13. The text of a lecture delivered at Nottingham University on 17 Mar. 1966.

[10] *T.A.*, p. 85.

[11] *T.A.*, p. 107.

function of knowledge is "to know the truth about reality." [12] Indeed,
the sort of trauma which faces Julian when he is urged to accept the
apparently diminutive "model" as symbolising reality is comparable to
that which faced Plato's man in the cave. For the world of reality is,
almost by definition, unattractive to those who have lived sufficiently
long with illusion. It is precisely for this reason, in fact, that the conspirators are forced to employ a more acceptable image of the real
world in the person of Alice.

Miss Alice is herself identifiable with the "model" castle, which is
actually referred to by the conspirators as "Alice"—a name which itself
means "truth." She is a surrogate, a fact which she explains to Julian in
a confession which can also be taken as Albee's justification for his resort to metaphor, "I have tried to be . . . *her*. No; I have tried to be
. . . what I thought she might, what might make you happy, what you
might use, as a . . . what? . . . we must . . . represent, draw pictures,
reduce or enlarge to . . . to what we can understand." [13] Thus, if
Julian cannot accept the God of society, the conspirators are prepared
to offer him a "true" God. For the Butler insists that there "is *something*. There is a 'true' God." It is the Lawyer, however, who explicitly
identifies it: "There is Alice, Julian. That can be understood. Only the
mouse in the model. Just that." [14]

In the moments before his death Julian comes finally to recognize
the inversion of his values which has resulted from his contact with
Alice. For as he looks at a phrenological head, which Albee has rather
pointedly left on stage throughout most of the play, he realises that
his compulsion has always been to grant reality only to abstractions; to
see man, in other words, solely in terms of this head with its eyes
focused on some far horizon (the afterlife) rather than as a creature of
flesh and blood existing in a concrete world.

> Is that the . . . awful humour? Art thou the true arms, when the
> warm flesh I touched . . . rested against, was . . . nothing? . . . Is
> thy stare the true look? . . . The ABSTRACT . . . REAL? THE REST? . . .
> FALSE? It is what I have wanted, have insisted on. Have nagged . . . for.
> IS THIS MY PRIESTHOOD, THEN? THIS WORLD?" [15]

Julian himself, for whom abstention from intimate human contact
has been a sworn article of faith, is left finally reconciled to the fact that

---

[12] Plato, *The Republic of Plato*, tr. F. M. Cornford (London 1955), p. 180.
[13] *T.A.*, p. 161.
[14] *T.A.*, p. 107.
[15] *T.A.*, pp. 188–9.

his priesthood is indeed in this world and that its whole object lies in making contact with the "warm flesh" of his fellow men.

Julian's death is pointedly a crucifixion, a martyrdom enacted against the model castle which is the epitome of reality and truth. Indeed one ending, later discarded, would have left him actually tied to the model. As he dies, in a reversal of his former "conversion," his cry to God now changes to a cry for Alice. At the same time his mind reverts to the image of the person shut up in the attic closet, and he admits, what he would not have admitted before, that "No one will come." [16] (In the original ending this closing scene was actually to have been played inside a closet—an idea which finally had to bow to theatrical practicality.) Julian also, arrives at a further realisation, one that might be taken both as the reason for his own retreat into illusion and as an explanation of Albee's own obsessive insistence on the necessity of violence. He comes to understand that "Consciousness . . . is pain." [17]

As Julian dies, the heartbeats which had reverberated with an increasing intensity suddenly cease as well—an audible confirmation that ultimately man is indeed his own God and the only supra-reality that which he creates himself. The secular evangelism of the conspirators has thus created its own saint in Julian, and they leave after covering the furniture with sheets in a way which is clearly intended to suggest the veiled images of Holy Week. Like Jerry before him, Julian has accepted a sacrifice which provides the basis for a new religion of man, which, if it grants no reality to metaphysical abstraction, does at least define the limits of human activity. For Albee clearly believes, with the novelist Ignazio Silone, that "The first sign of manhood is a shedding of abstractions in an effort to press toward 'an intimate opening on to the reality of others.' " [18]

If the symbolic pattern of *Tiny Alice* is essentially Platonic, the dilemma which that pattern highlights is, as Albee has shown in his previous plays, one central to modern society. It is interesting to see, in fact, just how closely Julian matches the archetypal neurotic in retreat from reality as outlined by a pioneer in psychology, Alfred Adler. The very precision of his parallel, indeed, tends to grant to Albee's creation the general application which is clearly his aim. Adler terms escapism "Safe-guarding through distance." His description of the neurotic fits Julian's situation precisely. His reference to the past, his concern with

16 *T.A.*, p. 176.
17 *T.A.*, p. 181.
18 R. W. B. Lewis, *The Picaresque Saint* (London 1960), p. 151.

death, and his choice of religion are all recognised by Adler as symptoms of this desire to "safeguard through distance."

> To think about the past is an unobtrusive, and therefore popular, means of shirking. Also, fear of death or disease. . . . The consolation of religion with the hereafter can have the same effect, by making a person see his actual goal only in the hereafter and the existence on earth as a very superfluous endeavour. . . .[19]

An American psychiatrist, Dr. Abraham Franzblau, reminds us that Freud himself had felt that religious dogma stemmed ultimately "from man's unwillingness to accept mortality, to recognize the rapacious cruelty of nature, or to sacrifice some of his libidinous gratifications for the help he needs from his fellow men." [20]

The title of Albee's play would seem to suggest that *The Collected Works of Lewis Carroll* should be necessary reading, and several critics have in fact been at pains to insist on its relevance. For clearly Alice's Wonderland, as an escape from "dull reality," can be seen as a parallel to Julian's wonderland of religion, in so far as it grows out of a similar unwillingness to accept the restrictions of reality. Moreover, the confrontation of reality and illusion, which lies at the heart of Albee's play, is achieved in Carroll with a symbol which, like Albee's, is essentially Platonic. But while Carroll's literally "tiny" Alice is a part of the illusory world, Albee's tiny Alice symbolises reality. If Carroll insists on returning his protagonist to the real world at the end of his book, it is, perhaps, not without a nostalgic glance back over his shoulder to his wonderland, however brutal that wonderland may at times appear. There is no such nostalgic glance in Albee.

Julian has to relinquish the abstraction which is his retreat from reality. In doing so he abandons the robes of the Church for the clothes of ordinary life, a change which symbolises his shift of identity. This assumption of identity as a function of an adopted role is reminiscent of Nigel Dennis's satire on the great abstractions of modern society, *Cards of Identity* (1956). Here, too, three conspirators effect a change of identity in a man lured to their "mansion" by the prospect of monetary gain—a change signified here, as in *Tiny Alice,* by a physical change of clothes. To Dennis, also, religion is one of those projections whereby man escapes from the immediate reality of his situation and accepts a ready-made identity. It is an escape, moreover, which

19 Alfred Adler, *The Individual Psychology of Alfred Adler,* ed. H. L. Ansbacher and R. R. Ansbacher (London 1958), p. 277.

20 A. N. Franzblau, "A Psychiatrist Looks at 'Tiny Alice,'" *Saturday Review,* 30 Jan. 1965, p. 39. [See p. 110 in this volume.]

implies a denial of intellect, as it does a denial of reality. In Dennis's ironical words, "God is worshipped as a solid only by backward people; once educated, the mind reaches out for what cannot be grasped, recognises only what cannot be seen: sophistry adores a vacuum" [21]; or, more succinctly, as he puts it in his unabashed satire on religion, *The Making of Moo* (1957), "You have nothing to lose but your brains." [22]

Once again, however, the writer whose work offers the closest parallel to Albee's is T. S. Eliot. In a real sense *Tiny Alice* can be seen as a prose version of *The Cocktail Party*. In this play Eliot had presented a similar conspiracy of three designed to "save," in this case, four people. Like Julian, these characters are

> stripped naked to their souls
> And can choose, whether to put on proper costumes
> Or huddle quickly into new disguises.[23]

Edward and Lavinia, who form the nucleus of an involved romantic tangle, choose to retreat into just such a disguise. Having been confronted with the real world, they reconcile themselves to their situation in a way which brings them to the verge of indifference. They

> Learn to avoid excessive expectation,
> Become tolerant of themselves and others
> Giving and taking, in the usual actions
> What there is to give and take. They do not repine;
> Are contented with the morning that separates
> And with the evening that brings together
> For casual talk before the fire
> Two people who do not understand each other
> Breeding children whom they do not understand
> and who will never understand them.[24]

Eliot is at pains to draw a clear distinction between this kind of soulless reconciliation and a genuine decision to face the fundamental reality of the human condition in order to construct some kind of meaningful response to it. Edward's mistress, Celia, does just this. She realises that she has been living in an essentially unreal world and comes to understand, as does Julian in Albee's play, that her version of reality has been

> only a projection
> . . . of something that I wanted—No, not *wanted*

[21] Nigel Dennis, *Two Plays and a Preface* (London 1958), p. 7.
[22] *Op. cit.*, p. 194.
[23] T. S. Eliot, *Collected Plays* (London 1962), p. 193.
[24] *Op. cit.*, p. 189.

—something I aspired to—
Something that I desperately wanted to exist.[25]

If she comes now to accept the stark horror of a world in which communication seems impossible, in which "everyone's alone," [26] in doing
so she also discovers her responsibility to love. It is this perception
which sets her on a path leading directly to her crucifixion—a fitting
climax to the life of an individual whose values differ so fundamentally
from those of society. When Julian faces his "crucifixion," it is with a
similar understanding of the true nature of reality and of the need to
acknowledge a commitment to his fellow man. In both cases the decision is celebrated by the conspirators with a champagne toast in a
sacrificial gesture in keeping with this martyrdom.

In *Tiny Alice,* therefore, Albee's apocalyptic vision, implied in *Who's
Afraid of Virginia Woolf?,* is more clearly defined. The abstract fear
of the former play is crystallised in Julian's perception of the terrifying
loneliness of man. Used to the projections of his own sensibilities, he
has to come to accept a diminution of his concept of reality. He also
has to accept his responsibility for creating his own identity and meaning. For Albee is insisting that man's freedom and identity ultimately
depend on his ability to discount reliance on an abstraction which is
the creation of his own metaphysical solitude. As Goetz had said in
Sartre's *Lucifer and the Lord* (1951), "God is the loneliness of man.
. . . If God exists, man is nothing." [27]

Albee has said that "the new theatre in the United States is going to
concern itself with the re-evaluation of the nature of reality and, therefore, it's going to move away from the naturalistic tradition." [28] *Tiny
Alice,* like *Who's Afraid of Virginia Woolf?* before it, is proof of
Albee's personal devotion to this principle. Indeed, when Alice makes
her first appearance dressed as an old crone, only to throw off her disguise and appear in her full beauty, this in itself is surely an indication of Albee's central purpose in a play which he himself has called
"a morality play about truth and illusion," [29] and which is clearly
dedicated to stripping the masks from religion, hypocrisy, materialism,
and cant.

25 *Op. cit.,* p. 154.
26 *Op. cit.,* p. 186.
27 Jean-Paul Sartre, *Lucifer and the Lord,* tr. Kitty Black (London 1952), p. 133.
28 Digby Diehl, "Edward Albee Interviewed by Digby Diehl," *Transatlantic Review,* No. 13 (Summer 1963), p. 62.
29 Thomas B. Markus, "Tiny Alice and Tragic Catharsis," *Educational Theatre
Journal,* xvii, p. 230.

Albee is concerned, then, with what Thomas Mann, in a slightly different sense, has called the "dark underside" of man, those areas in his life, that is, which he tries desperately to conceal even from himself. For Albee, like Pirandello and later Genet, is all too aware of the internal and external pressures on the individual to escape from doubt, ambiguity, and uncertainty by retreating into a pre-determined role— whether that role be shaped by the Church or by society. For as a clearly defined functionary man feels that he is no longer adrift in a purposeless world, but is part of what he is prepared to accept as a meaningful order. Albee is finally concerned with this individual's response to seeing himself without a mask. He is concerned with penetrating behind the façade of public assurance to the true sense of fear, desertion, and real courage which he sees as lying at the heart of the human predicament. This, in a sense, is that "dissolution of the ego" which Joseph Wood Krutch has seen as the essential subject of contemporary literature. To Albee, though, it is essential to dismantle the ego, not in order to find the source of its psychosis, but rather to discover the foundation of its strength. Like the protagonist of Ralph Ellison's *Invisible Man,* Julian has to dive down into the depths of his consciousness before he can emerge again with a valid response to his surroundings.

But this is essentially an internalised drama—one which is of necessity acted out within the mind of the protagonist. This in itself accounts for Albee's move here towards monologue. For when Albee describes *Tiny Alice* as "something small enclosed in something else," [30] he is not only referring to the central symbol of the castle, but also to the structure of a play which can be legitimately seen as a mono-drama taking place entirely within Julian's own tormented mind. To the extent that this is true, a great deal of the obscurity and ambiguity which lies at the heart of the play can be seen as a direct expression of Julian's own bewilderment—a fact which nevertheless fails to redeem the confusions of a play which all too often substitutes technical facility for genuine engagement. Where Pirandello had succeeded in translating his metaphysical conundrums into flesh and blood, *Tiny Alice* remains for the most part a merely ingenious exercise. Pirandello justifiably boasted that he had converted the intellect into passion. In the place of passion Albee offers only refined anguish.

In *Who's Afraid of Virginia Woolf?* Albee had attempted to com-

---

[30] Lee Baxandall, "The Theatre of Edward Albee," *Tulane Drama Review,* ix (1965), p. 36.

municate beneath the level of language by creating a sub-structure of imagery. In *Tiny Alice*, his precise control of this imagery ultimately breaks down, and instead of operating as an endemic part of the play, as did the fantasy child in his former play, it becomes little more than a substitute for dramatic action. Indeed, Albee becomes every bit as inept as Tennessee Williams, who has always had a penchant for littering his stage with any number of highly significant objects, from dried up fountains and anatomical charts to iguanas. While the castle probably represents a high-point in mishandled symbolism, perhaps the single most painful symbol is the phrenological head which is left on stage for most of the play, apparently so that Julian may remark on it in the final scene. One effect of this rather gross mishandling of imagery was that audiences tended to be thrown into varying degrees of confusion; and, while reviewers responded to its obvious power and originality, they likewise found its meaning somewhat elusive. Further, Albee's admission, in the author's note which precedes the published play, that *"Tiny Alice* is less opaque in reading than it would be in any single viewing," is an incredible confession for a dramatist to make. For in choosing to write for the theatre he has presumably accepted the challenge of communicating directly to an audience, and in this he has patently failed. He is, it appears, clearly not prepared to make any concessions to the audience—not even those made necessary by the nature of drama.

His failure in *Tiny Alice*, moreover, makes one doubt what is clearly one of the play's central premises. For the assumption that the model is more "real" than the castle itself has a further implication. It implies that art itself is more valid than an inauthentic life founded on nothing more secure than fear and illusion. In the rarefied atmosphere of *Tiny Alice*, one is far from convinced.

In his own defence Albee has suggested that an audience might require several visits in order to fathom the play's various depths. Unfortunately this is not borne out by the experience of one man. John Gielgud, who played Julian, found that time did not make the play any more comprehensible for him. Perhaps, therefore, there was more than a little truth in the answer which Albee offered to Gielgud's incomprehension: "I know you want to know what the play's about, John, but I don't know yet, so I can't say." [31]

31 R. S. Stewart, "John Gielgud and Edward Albee Talk about the Theatre," *Atlantic Monthly*, CCXV (1965), pp. 67–8. [Reprinted in this volume, p. 112.]

Albee Decorates an Old House:
A Delicate Balance

by Robert Brustein

Edward Albee's recent work poses a number of problems for the reviewer, one of them being that it is virtually impossible to discuss it without falling into repetition. Looking over the anthology of pieces I have written about his annual procession of plays, I discover that I am continually returning to two related points: that his plays have no internal validity and that they are all heavily dependent upon the style of other dramatists. At the risk of boring the reader, I am forced to repeat these judgments about *A Delicate Balance*. The fourth in a series of disappointments that Albee has been turning out since *Who's Afraid of Virginia Woolf?*, this work, like its predecessors, suffers from a borrowed style and a hollow center. It also suggests that Albee's talent for reproduction has begun to fail him until by now the labels on his lendings are all but exposed to public view. Reviewers have already noted the stamp of T. S. Eliot on *A Delicate Balance* (a nametag that was somewhat more subtly imprinted on *Tiny Alice* as well), and it is quite true that Albee, like Eliot before him, is now trying to invest the conventional drawing-room comedy with metaphysical significance. But where Eliot was usually impelled by a religious vision, Albee seems to be stimulated by mere artifice, and the result is emptiness, emptiness, emptiness.

A Delicate Balance is, to my mind, a very bad play—not as bad as *Malcolm*, which had a certain special awfulness all its own, but boring and trivial nevertheless. It is also the most remote of Albee's plays—so far removed from human experience, in fact, that one wonders if Albee is not letting his servants do his living for him. Although the action is supposed to take place in suburban America—in the living room and

"Albee Decorates an Old House: *A Delicate Balance*" (editor's title). From Robert Brustein, *The Third Theatre*. Copyright © 1966 by Robert Brustein. Reprinted by permission of Alfred A. Knopf, Inc., and Jonathan Cape Ltd.

conservatory of an upper middle-class family—the environment is more that of the English landed gentry as represented on the West End before the Osborne revolution. Leatherbound books sit on library shelves, elbowing copies of *Horizon;* brandy and anisette and martinis are constantly being decanted between, over, and under bits of dialogue; the help problem becomes an object of concern, as well as problems of friendship, marriage, sex, and the proper attitude to take toward pets; and characters discuss their relationships in a lapidary style as far from modern speech as the whistles of a dolphin.

The failure of the language, actually, is the most surprising failure of the play, especially since Albee's control of idiom has usually been his most confident feature. Here, on the other hand, banal analogies are forced to pass for wisdom: "Friendship is something like a marriage, is it not, Tobias, for better or for worse?" The plot is signaled with all the subtlety of a railroad brakeman rerouting a train: "Julia is coming home. She is leaving Douglas, which is no surprise to me." A relaxed idiom is continually sacrificed to clumsy grammatical accuracy: "You are a guest," observes one character, to which the other replies, "As you." If colloquialisms are spoken, they are invariably accompanied by self-conscious apologies: One character drinks "like the famous fish," while another observes, "You're copping out, as they say." Empty chatter is passed off as profound observation with the aid of irrelevant portentous subordinate clauses: "Time happens, I suppose, to people. Everything becomes too late finally." And the play ends with one of those vibrato rising-sun lines familiar from at least a dozen such evenings: "Come now, we can begin the day."

It is clear that Albee has never heard such people talk, he has only read plays about them, and he has not retained enough from his reading to give his characters life. More surprisingly, he has not even borrowed creatively from his own work, for although a number of Albee's usual strategies are present in *A Delicate Balance,* they do not function with much cogency. One character, for example, tells of his difficulties with a cat that no longer loved him—a tale that recalls a similar tale about a dog in *The Zoo Story*—but here the narrative is no more than a sentimental recollection. Similarly, a dead child figures in this work, as in so many Albee plays, but it has no organic relevance to the action and seems introduced only to reveal the sexual hang-ups of the protagonist and to fill up time.

Too much of the play, in fact, seems purely decorative: there simply isn't enough material here to make up a full evening. *A Delicate*

Balance concerns a family of four—a passive husband, an imperious wife, an alcoholic sister-in-law, and a much divorced daughter—whose problems are exacerbated when they are visited by some married friends. This couple has just experienced a nameless terror in their home, and when they move in on the family for comfort and security, a delicate balance is upset, all the characters learning that terror is infectious, like the plague. This plot has a nice touch of mystery about it, but its main consequence is to move various sexually estranged couples into each other's rooms after various impassioned dialogues. What finally puzzles the will is how very little Albee now thinks can make up a play: a few confessions, a few revelations, a little spookiness, and an emotional third-act speech.

Alan Schneider's production is stiff and pedestrian. One senses discomfort in the staging as well as in the performances: these are not roles that actors fill with pleasure. Rosemary Murphy has some vigor as the alcoholic sister-in-law, coming on like one of those sardonic (male) drunks that used to appear in the plays of Philip Barry, but like the other performers, she has a difficult time recovering the portentous rhythms of the play when she stumbles over a line. Hume Cronyn, usually one of our most dependable actors, is dry and uninteresting as the father; Jessica Tandy is delicate but high-pitched as the mother; and Marian Seldes as the daughter is vocally and physically angular. The director occasionally tries for an effect, as when he arranges four ladies with their coffee cups in the attitude of an Eliot chorus, but most of the time we are spared such tableaux and the stage is left as empty as the play. It is an emptiness that no amount of activity can fill. *A Delicate Balance* is an old house which an interior decorator has tried to furnish with reproductions and pieces bought at auction. But the house has never been lived in and the wind murmurs drily through its corridors.

A Vision of Baal

A Delicate Balance

by Anne Paolucci

The entire repertory of dramatic voices and symbolic themes traced up to this point emerges in a *pianissimo* of subtle harmonies in *A Delicate Balance,* the most deceptively conventional of Albee's plays to date.

Its setting recalls the social malaise of *Who's Afraid of Virginia Woolf?*—suburbia at its best, which is to say, at its worst. There is nothing here, however, of the academic and intellectual pretensions which intensity the action of the earlier play; there is no one even remotely resembling Martha and George in their manic-depressive confrontations. The people in *A Delicate Balance,* like those in *All Over,* seem, by contrast, commonplace and stale, mediocre even. They might be Honeys and Nicks who have settled for a less competitive routine of life, which they can sustain by sheer inertia. The cast, in other words, like the furniture of the setting, is more polished, more expensive and tasteful, but also less interesting, at first glance. And, in the action too, the excitement of raw confrontations is missing; things run relatively smoothly; even the one big crisis of the play seems to be in a low key. Throughout there is an insistence upon dignity and restraint as sheer convention; even insults are quietly civilized.

This calm surface is the most beguiling and misleading of Albee's fictions. Things are and remain what they seem, and yet—Clare's alcoholism and Julia's divorces are more than a poor attempt to inject nervous excitement into a rather ordinary setting; Agnes's forced wit and Tobias's pompous propriety are not simply low-level repartee; the play is only superficially a sarcastic commentary on the idle rich and the vices born of leisure. As a total experience, it is as impressive as any of the earlier plays, although it is only fair to note that the psychopathic sparring of Martha and George, the obsessive concern of Jerry for Peter, the superhuman efforts of Brother Julian to grasp comfort and love are, on the surface, more satisfying dramatically. Jerry's total sacrifice, Martha's consuming passion, Julian's terrible ordeal—though farfetched in terms of ordinary experience—move us immediately; Agnes's fear of madness and Tobias's dread of exposure at having to tell his friends they can't move in permanently, though *probable* enough, seem to fall short of a soul-shattering crisis. In this play, dramatic tension is even less compelling than it is in *All Over,* where the imminent death of the Husband-Father-Lover-Friend forces the protagonists together in an artificial unity which—despite its tenuous nature—is at once believable and acceptable, a familiar and perfectly reasonable convention.

And yet, in *A Delicate Balance* Albee seems to insist on such a crisis. To top it all, he drags in as catalyst—to force the action to a climax —something called the Terror, which he is inconsiderate enough to leave an uncompromising blank. The mystery—one might be tempted to conclude—is not that grown people like Edna and Harry could be frightened by an empty word, but that a mature and experienced dramatist like Albee should have been satisfied with such a rotten gimmick.

Ironically, audiences have usually enjoyed the play as good entertainment, as a kind of thing Noel Coward might have done with the same dramatis personae. Its neat and not-too-demanding dramatic structure is easy to follow and—except for the one puzzling element already alluded to—raises no unanswerable questions. Still, Harry and Edna are not extraneous to the action; their Terror is not a *deus ex machina* as some have suggested. And this *does* raise a puzzling question: could the author of *Who's Afraid of Virginia Woolf?* and *Tiny Alice* really have been satisfied with well-worn clichés about life in the suburbs?

With the possible exception of *All Over,* this play is perhaps the most consistently "realistic" and uniform of Albee's works. Except for the Terror which Edna and Harry insist on, the realistic representation is never seriously threatened. But the exception is, of course, the central event of the action: either Albee failed as a dramatist or we must look at it in a different light.

The Terror that animates Edna and Harry never really succeeds in

damaging the illusory calm of the action because it is refused admission
into the house. But that refusal is, in effect, a shattering confrontation,
in which each member of the household is forced to examine his conscience and to confess his true motives. Tobias, as head of the family,
must choose between self-sacrifice and self-control; Agnes must exert
her will to direct Tobias in his final choice; Julia and Clare must recognize their weaknesses for what they are and settle for comfortable
egoism. In its probing of intentions and its exposure of human limitations, the play is equal to Albee's other brilliant accomplishments, up
to and including *Tiny Alice*. In rejecting the test forced upon them,
the protagonists reject their better selves; grasping, vicious, and even
naïve at the beginning, they all end up damned.

The Terror, in fact, is not an external event, no surprise. It already
exists in Tobias's household in a variety of guises. Agnes understands
immediately what it's all about because she has already experienced it.
For her, it is the threat of insanity—a threat which she describes
pleasantly as a kind of joke:

> What I find most astonishing—aside from that belief of mine, which
> never ceases to surprise me by the very fact of its surprising lack of
> unpleasantness, the belief that I might very easily—as they say—lose
> my mind one day, not that I suspect I am about to, or am even . . .
> nearby . . . for I'm not that sort; merely, that it is not beyond . . .
> happening: some gentle loosening of the moorings sending the baloon
> adrift—and I think that is the only outweighing thing: adrift; the
> . . . becoming a stranger in . . . the world, quite . . . uninvolved, for
> I never see it as violent, only a drifting. . . . But I could never do it—
> go adrift—for what would become of you? Still, what I find most as-
> tonishing, aside, as I said, from that speculation—and I wonder, too,
> sometimes, if I am the only one of you to admit to it: not that *I* may
> go mad, but that each of you wonders if each of *you* might not—

The motif reappears at the end of the play, framing the action as a
precarious act of will, a conscious decision to reject the easy way out,
the "gentle loosening of the moorings." The Terror for Agnes is not
oblivion, but the awareness that it's there, lying in wait for her. It is
not "violent"—but like the action of the entire play, the very lack of
violence is the measure of its depth. One must be constantly alert to
avoid drifting off. For Agnes, the task is all-important, for without her
the others would soon destroy themselves.

Madness lurks within the house long before the "terror" is an-
nounced. Agnes jokes about it, but it is a real terror. Clare, the nerve-

center of the group, teeters on the brink of destruction, unable to tear herself away; Julia, self-centered and immature, keeps a safe distance but feels the pull; Tobias has seen something of the darkness but has deliberately chosen the comparative safety of habit and routine; Agnes has faced it and has decided to keep to level ground, although—as she herself makes perfectly clear—she is all too often sorely tempted to leap into the abyss.

Agnes is the refuge for the others. She is just as vulnerable as they, but her will is strong and refuses to buckle under. She urges Tobias to consider the emotional health of his family in making his decision about Harry and Edna. It is not cruelty but love which prompts her to reject her best friends. In her willful determination to protect her own, she guides Tobias into the same kind of rejection—although she is just as ready to go along with some other decision, should he decide to come out of his lethargy. The outcome is sensible but sad. Friendship, after all, is—or should be—sacred.

The Terror which threatens to destroy Agnes's world—unlike the psychological and religious forces at work in the earlier plays—is left undefined. It is not, however, without content; nor is its uncertain nature the vagueness which invites indiscriminate interpretation by each member of the audience. These two extremes suggest themselves, of course; but Albee has given us a very concrete statement about them, in his insistence that Edna and Harry never be mistaken for or drawn into the center of the action. Their inexpressible Terror must be understood by reflection, *indirectly*. It is held up, in the course of the action, to a number of articulate mirrors which are the tangible fears of the different members of the household. The Terror of Edna and Harry becomes in that spectrum the fears of Julia, the emptiness of Clare, the withdrawal of Tobias, the implicit madness of Agnes, a series of nightmares which never break through the veneer of appearances. In this light, the play becomes a Pirandellian experience, a *happening* on many levels.

The Terror which Edna and Harry drag with them into their friends' house is all the diversified horrors of life. Their coming shocks the others into frightening awareness of the death that lies in each of them. Their entrance is the occasion for a critical reassessment, on the part of each of the others, of their vices, their shortcomings, their lies and egoism. Julia cannot cope with the challenge; Clare simply reaffirms her preference for oblivion through drink; Tobias comes to the surface of the truth for a moment, only to confess his inadequacy; Agnes recognizes the challenge but knows it is not her decision. Madness opens and closes the play and comes to the very threshold of the dramatic action, but it never really breaks loose from its moorings. What havoc it could wreak is barely suggested in the emotional paralysis of Edna and Harry and in the frightening spectacle of Tobias struggling with his conscience.

Terror takes on as many forms as there are personalities to recognize it. Its simplest reflection is in Julia, the sexless symbol of sex—at once victim and torturer, child and woman. Julia returns home after each broken marriage (she has reached her fourth) to find strength and reassurance among her own. The paradox is obvious: home is a mirage, a long-lost dream, the dead past, and in choosing to return to it, Julia is merely aggravating her already serious emotional difficulties. Tobias cannot help her; in his own way, he loves his child, perhaps suffers with her, but he cannot overcome his inertia long enough to reach out to her in a meaningful way. He steers clear of unpleasantness, incapable of sharing and perfecting his love through sacrifice. Julia is, in a sense, a monster he has created. He cannot help her and never will, just as he cannot help Agnes who, in her moment of need, was gently but firmly thrust aside. In her search for love, Julia merely reflects her mother's own disappointing experience. Agnes understands Julia's predicament and therefore does not presume to judge her. All she can do is be there when Julia returns, nurturing the illusion of authority and stability, maintaining some kind of order, the familiar routine which is Julia's only hold on sanity. When she comes home it is to a sterile past, as a wayward child corrupted by her own vices and seeking—in parental authority—a substitute for responsibility. In her own room, she abdicates decisions of her own. She indulges in tantrums and welcomes the firm hand which puts them down. The hand should have been Tobias's, but it is Agnes's. Julia is doomed to a perpetual search for identity, coming to rest periodically in a naïve optimism, symbolized by the familiar room of her adolescence. When that familiar environment is invaded by Edna and Harry, her latent hysteria bursts forth. Julia is the most pathetic, the weakest, the naïvest, of the tribe. She is one extreme of the spectrum.

At the other extreme is Clare, the ancient Sibyl, who spares no one in her flashes of insight—not even herself. Alcoholism fires her imagination and her cruelty (she is a weaker sister of Martha); she is at her best —and worst—when drunk, most contemptuous of the world, wittiest, most ironic and critical. Her utterances have the attraction of oracular prophecy. Truth ravishes her and she, in turn, lashes out with destructive fury at those around her. She probes Tobias's weaknesses, jars him into remembering what he would much rather forget; like the distant gods, she cannot sympathize for long or forgive or identify with anyone else completely. Her ironic detachment—especially with Tobias —is her image of superiority, her pathetic self-confidence. She loves Tobias and wishes—she says—that Agnes were dead, so Tobias could turn to *her*. It's a dream that will never be put to a test, for Clare needs Agnes as much as the others do. Without her sister, Clare's illusion of independence will be completely shattered; she is too far gone to have anything to offer on her own, and Tobias is too distant to accept the gift of anyone's love. Agnes allows her to indulge in the dream, for Clare's terror is the fear of losing her identity. The coming of Edna and Harry threatens her as much as it threatens the rest of the famliy, but her stoic bravado keeps her from collapsing under the strain. This crisis, like all the others, will also pass. Prosaic routine will take over again, will restore their illusion of meaningful action.

Tobias alone rises to a conscious, decisive confrontation. His story of the cat—like Jerry's narrative of the dog, in *The Zoo Story* and Julian's confession of his experience with the unknown woman of the asylum in *Tiny Alice*—sums up in a single, realistic symbol the central crisis of the play. The story rises out of Tobias's painful awareness of his inability to say or do anything that could settle Julia's problem. His failure with his daughter reminds him of his failure with the cat. He has no words of wisdom to impart, so why try?

> If I saw some point to it, I might—if I saw some reason, chance. If I thought I might . . . break through to her, and say, "Julia . . . ," but then what would I say? "Julia . . ." Then, nothing.

It isn't Julia's peculiar difficulty that he can't solve; every difficulty is painful to him, beyond him. He has shied away from difficulties all his life; his problems are buried deep within him. Julia's demands remind him of his own demands on the cat he once owned and loved—the cat which stopped loving him one day and which, out of sheer spite, he had put to death. But the memory haunts him. How can love stop? Can it be taken away? What does it all mean? How does one regain lost love? And, if it cannot be regained, how does one adjust to the terrible fact?

> One night—I was *fixed* on it now—I had her in the room with me, and on my lap for the . . . what, the fifth time the same evening, and she

lay there, with her back to me, and she wouldn't purr, and I *knew;* I
knew she was just waiting till she could get down, and I said, "Damn
you, you like me; God damn it, you stop this! I haven't *done* anything
to you." And I shook her; I had my hands around her shoulders, and I
shook her . . . and she bit me; hard; and she hissed at me. And so I
hit her. With my open hand, I hit her, smack, right across the head.
I . . . I *hated* her!

The story of the cat, like the story of the dog in *The Zoo Story,* is the
emotional turning point of the play. Much has been said about Albee's
admirable storytelling technique, but what needs to be stressed further
is the fact that the stories are always an integral part of the action.
They are always the key to meaning, significantly placed to provide the
greatest dramatic tension. It is Julia's predicament, in this case, which
draws the story of the cat from Tobias—just as the story of the landlady's dog, in *The Zoo Story,* rises out of Jerry's efforts to "reach" Peter.
The story of the cat reminds Tobias of his egoism and indifference. He
preferred to have the cat destroyed than to suffer in his vanity.

In the midst of the spell which the story has cast, Edna and Harry
make their startling appearance. The juxtaposition of events cannot be
ignored: the story of the cat is the "text"—the larger action, the explication or lesson.

A number of analogies, in fact, suggest themselves. In his relationship with Julia, Tobias takes on the characteristics of the cat; the same
relationship is evident in his attitude toward Agnes. With Harry, Tobias is forced to live through the traumatic reversal again: he cannot
bring himself to give the trust and love demanded by friendship. On a
most profound though secret level of logic, the cat was justified; in his
confrontation with Harry, Tobias finally begins to understand something of the mysterious motivations which prompted the cat to act as
she did. Love should, *must* inspire a return of love: that's what Dante's
Francesca says to justify her adulterous love of Paolo. On that level of
"higher" morality, Tobias's cat obviously failed him. But hasn't Tobias
failed Agnes according to that same rule—and doesn't he now fail
Harry in the same way? Detached and unfeeling (unlike Francesca),
the cat was ready to lash out at Tobias—but Tobias, as husband and
friend, has been just as guilty and just as cruel. Agnes has forgiven
him, we know; and Harry says he understands. But Tobias himself
neither forgives nor understands himself—just as he could not understand the cat.

> She and I had lived together and been, well, you know, friends, and
> . . . there was no *reason*. And I hated her for that. I hated her, well, I
> suppose because I was being accused of something, of . . . failing. But
> I hadn't been cruel, by design; if I'd been neglectful, well, my life was
> . . . I resented it. I resented having a . . . being judged. Being be-
> trayed.

Even now, he is not being cruel by design, but the effect is exactly as if
he had been. It is the silent judgment he cannot abide; instinctively, he
knows he has betrayed his friends.

Tobias's analysis of the cat's reversal of feeling is precise and devastat-
ing, for it applies transparently to his own behavior toward those who
love him. The appearance of Harry and Edna, who force their friendship to a test, provides the detailed gloss to the story of the cat. Their
impossible demands—like his insistence that the cat return his affection—drive Tobias to impotent fury against himself. Harry has a right
to insist on his due—a true friend is ready for anything, or should be—
but Tobias can only lash out in frustration, as the cat had. "Do you
want us here, Tobias?" Harry insists; and Tobias can only repeat, "You
came here." Harry instinctively understands; habit and good breeding
will heal the breach; but Tobias can't stop there. He has recognized the
old test. The moment is full of ironic justice. He insists on Harry's taking what is rightfully his: "YES! OF COURSE! I WANT YOU HERE!
I HAVE BUILT THIS HOUSE! I WANT YOU IN IT! I WANT
YOUR PLAGUE! YOU'VE GOT SOME TERROR WITH YOU?
BRING IT IN!" What he really feels doesn't matter. "DON'T WE
LOVE EACH OTHER?" he asks miserably, hoping that Harry will
take what he *can* give and not ask the impossible of him.

> I DON'T WANT YOU HERE!
> YOU ASKED?!
> NO! I DON'T
>
> BUT BY CHRIST YOU'RE GOING TO
> STAY HERE!
> YOU'VE GOT THE RIGHT!
> THE RIGHT!

Tobias is ready to make good on a forty-year friendship. He insists on
it with the same passionate energy he expended on the cat.

> BY GOD YOU'RE GOING TO TAKE IT!
> DO YOU HEAR ME?!

> YOU BRING YOUR TERROR AND YOU COME IN HERE AND
>   YOU LIVE WITH US!
> YOU BRING YOUR PLAGUE!
> YOU STAY WITH US!
> I DON'T WANT YOU HERE!
> I DON'T LOVE YOU!
> BUT BY GOD . . . YOU STAY!!

Harry, like the cat, recognizes the imposition and refuses Tobias's offer. Love should be spontaneous and generous, make no demands or conditions. Tobias has failed the test again; and Harry gracefully withdraws.

The solution is less dramatic than the painful separation of *The Zoo Story* or the sacrifice of *Tiny Alice*, but just as terrible. In abdicating his responsibility, Tobias withdraws into frustrated loneliness. "I tried," he says when it is all over, "I was honest." He has settled for the illusion of peace. The ordeal, the Terror, is reduced to conventional proportions and buried with all the other failures of the past. Honesty has come and gone, and Tobias is once more in the limbo of the impotent with Clare and Julia. He has survived the Terror, but defeat will continue to plague him.

It is Agnes who quietly and efficiently takes command when the shouting is over, easing Tobias into the old detachment, the quiet routine which he craves. Agnes provides the clues to the interpretation of events. Her opening allusion to madness gives us the theme in its simplest form. Sanity is the necessity imposed on her. She accepts the world as defined by the others around her, not because she really prefers it that way, but because she truly loves and is prepared to give what they need. Her deceptive calm is an act of sheer will—the painful equilibrium between a Dionysian abandonment and an Apollonian restraint. She forces others to hold their own: Clare must fight back if she is to retain her identity; Julia must be scolded and comforted alternately; Tobias must be spared the emotional demands he cannot fulfill. She molds their lives into a predictable routine, reducing even the vices of the household to familiar "cliché" excesses.

Tobias is the only real challenge. What she does for Clare and Julia is unquestioned habit; but she can never take Tobias for granted or respond to his needs automatically. In her relationship with Tobias, she displays exquisite tact. Even her desperate appeal to his family responsibility, at the crucial moment when Terror threatens to move in, is full of loving tenderness. She doesn't challenge Tobias's professed love for his friends, although she recognizes it as a sentimental abstraction; she never resorts to bitterness or irony, although she has good reason to; she never takes advantage of the situation at the expense of Tobias's dignity. In spite of her quicker instincts and her better judgment, she insists that Tobias make the decision regarding Harry and Edna—convention demands it and psychological necessity dictates it. Here, as in the past, she is ready to accept whatever he decides. Her own preferences don't matter.

What she does is marshal the relevant facts for Tobias's benefit. The decision cannot be based on sentimentality or personal feeling. Tobias is not alone; the health of the entire household is at stake. Clare might survive the "invasion" ("the walking wounded often are, the least susceptible"), but what of Julia? What about Tobias himself? She sums up the case with a genial analogy:

> Let me tell you something about disease . . . mortal illness; you either are immune to it . . . or you fight it. If you are immune, you wade right in, you treat the patient until he either lives, or dies of it. But if you are *not* immune, you risk infection. Ten centuries ago—and even less—the treatment was quite simple . . . burn them. Burn their bodies, burn their houses, burn their clothes—and move to another town, if you were enlightened. But now, with modern medicine, we merely isolate; we quarantine, we ostracize—if we are not immune ourselves, or unless we are saints. So, your night-long vigil, darling, your reasoning in the cold, pure hours, has been over the patient, and not the illness. It is not Edna and Harry who have come to us—our friends—it is a disease.

Neither inertia nor grand gestures will solve the problem, cure the disease. If the others are immune, there is nothing to fear. Edna and Harry can stay as long as they wish. But if Julia and Clare and Tobias and Agnes are not immune, then they must get rid of the disease, the Terror—unless they are all prepared to be destroyed by it. Agnes is willing to take the risk of infection: "We're bound to die of something . . . soon, or in a while. Or shall we burn them out, rid ourselves of it all . . . and wait for the next invasion." But Tobias is neither Jerry nor Brother Julian. He has already made his choice; he has long since "isolated" those suffering from the disease. He has never waded in. In his own emotional life, Clare, Julia, and Agnes have been effectively quarantined. His solution to the Terror is perfectly consistent with everything else he has ever done.

Tobias is neither immune nor endowed with sainthood. His protestations of loyalty and friendship are mere bravado, though he means well. The choice Agnes has put to him so dramatically is an academic one; she knows perfectly well what Tobias will do. Agnes has already gone through the worst; nothing can either surprise or disappoint her. She, of all the members of the household, is "immune."

Agnes is the subtle chorus of the play, expanding and reinforcing Clare's oracular flashes of insight. But she is by no means detached from the action around her. The demands on her are all too real; she cannot indulge in indifference or in self-righteous sentimentality. It is up to her to keep things in check, to keep her world from falling apart. The little daily crises are safety valves which keep her from "drifting" off. She is the strongest person in the play—not because she is inspired or clairvoyant, but because she simply is dependable. Like Captain Mc-Whirr in Conrad's *Typhoon,* she lives through the Terror because of sheer constancy and habit. Like a Dürer *Melencolia,* she has taken on the job of creating order, molding reality into an illusion of peace. She is the restrained power of love turned into Pirandellian strength of will. She has no choice, for love too is a kind of disease and demands certain labors and cares. Tobias must be guided through his dilemma in a way that will not destroy him. Agnes is not domineering Mommy, but a wise Martha. She cannot indulge in Tobias's withdrawal into religious metaphors: "The inn is full—it's rather . . . Godlike, if I may presume: to look at it all, reconstruct, with such . . . de*tach*ment, see your*self,* you, Julia . . . Look at it all . . . play it out again, watch." But his role, Agnes reminds him, cannot be that of an observer. He must direct the action, tell others what to do. "We don't decide the route," says Agnes, speaking as representative of the "dependent" family. As such, she can only implement his decision.

> The reins we hold! It's a team of twenty horses, and we sit there, and we watch the road and check the leather . . . if our . . . man is so disposed. But there are things we do not do.

The decisions, in fact, have always been made by Tobias. It's his prerogative and duty. It was Tobias who decided they would not have another child, after their son's death. It was Tobias who decided that he and Agnes must not live as man and wife for fear of the intimacy which such a relationship would demand of him and which he was no longer disposed to give. It was Tobias who forced her slowly into a sterile life, taking to his "own sweet room" to avoid all temptation and silent recriminations. It was Tobias who allowed Julia to slide. It was Tobias who accepted Clare into the select circle of disillusioned human beings, as a kind of buffer between himself and Agnes. In all these decisions, Agnes accepted the "route" and helped him to his destination.

Agnes's will is strong, but not independent. Her task is to prod Tobias into articulating what he has already deep inside him. In her impact on Tobias, she—with Clare and Julia—resembles the witches in *Macbeth*—an image which Tobias himself hits on: "you'll all sit down and watch me carefully; smoke your pipes and stir the cauldron; watch." Clare in her demonic and vicious sparring, Julia in her fits of temper, Agnes in her restrained madness, mirror Tobias's own confusion. In them, his contradictory motives take demonic shape and assume demonic purpose. Like the witches in Shakespeare's play, they reflect those insights he would prefer not to acknowledge in himself. What Tobias does, in the end, like Macbeth, is truly and completely his own doing; the three women—like oracular apparitions—simply forge the moment of choice, trimming away all irrelevancies and excuses. Agnes, Clare, and Julia give Tobias the demonic courage he needs to assume the burden of decision and reveal himself in his true weakness. They are squeezed together, all of them, in a mysterious vise:

> Not even separation; that is taken care of, and in life: the gradual . . . demise of intensity, the private occupations, the substitutions. We become allegorical, my darling Tobias, as we grow older. The individuality we hold so dearly sinks into crotchet; we see ourselves by those we bring into it all, either by mirror or rejection, honor or fault.

In the trio of women, Tobias has constantly before him the frustrated resolutions of his egoism. In them he lives out his insufficiencies, the defects of his will. They are the voices of his conscience, his potential vices, and his inner madness. Like Macbeth, he would like to think of them as *causes* driving him into action—but the truth is that they really echo his perverted hopes. They are not external forces, but his own disguised intentions; not the ugliness outside him, but his own paralyzing limitations.

The beauty of the play lies in the realistic treatment of these subtle but powerful suggestions. There is little here of the immediate, palpable mystery of *Tiny Alice* or of the shattering psychological tensions of *Who's Afraid of Virginia Woolf?* From the very beginning, *A Delicate Balance* insists on "normality"—but it is the "normality" which results from a dynamic equilibrium of forces subdued and held in check. The unruffled surface is the draining of emotion; the entire play, a sustained metaphor.

To stop at a literal or obvious meaning (a play about the vices of suburbia or about the excesses of a materialistic society) is like summing up *Macbeth* as the story of a man who kills his king in order to take over the throne. Beyond the facts of the story, in both, is the struggle to transform reality into the image of the will. Where the will is corrupt or uncertain, it will project corruption and uncertainty. Tobias, like Macbeth, nurtures certain private ambitions, but he cannot articulate them as creatures of his will—and when they are finally given shape, he does not acknowledge them at once, hoping to trammel up the consequences if possible, jump the peace to come for the serenity of here and now. His partner in weakness—like Macbeth's partner in greatness—has dedicated her energies to helping him accomplish his ends. But Agnes, like Lady Macbeth, can go only so far. At the heart of darkness, Tobias—like Shakespeare's hero—must stand alone to face the terror of the completed deed. In Tobias, we catch a glimpse of the destructive Gorgon which turns love and trust into madness. In Agnes, we have a candid statement of its potential threat; but unlike Lady Macbeth, Agnes wins the battle against demonic heroism.

The action of the play moves from symbol to explication in a series of ever-growing circles of meaning, which is Albee's characteristic approach to dramatic exposition. Out of this dialectic—the kaleidoscopic superimposition of intention and result, statement and insight, truth and paradox—comes the illusion of reality, which is always a delicate balance of literal and metaphorical, familiar particulars and poetic image.

Box and *Quotations from Chairman Mao Tse-Tung:* Albee's Diptych

by C. W. E. Bigsby

In the last dozen or so years Edward Albee has delivered a number of theatrical shocks to a Broadway scarcely renowned for its fearless commitment to experimentation. As a result, the metaphysical enigmas of *Tiny Alice* and the "surreal" images of *Malcolm* were both greeted with a mixture of suspicion and incomprehension. Though the 1968 production of two related one-act plays, *Box* and *Quotations from Chairman Mao Tse-Tung,* fared somewhat better, these too strained critical responses forged in the Ibsenesque crucible of the American theatre. Walter Kerr responded with predictable bemused boredom while Jack Kroll, who produced a sensitive assessment of the two plays in his *Newsweek* review, missed the essential ambivalence of Albee's stance. Equally misleading was Michael Rutenberg's description of the work as "another protest play",[1] in his book *Edward Albee: Playwright in Protest,* for it is precisely Albee's unwillingness to be contained by such casual labels which is the source of the evocative quality of plays which are concerned with debating the function of art and the individual's responsibility in a world increasingly scornful of public and personal realities.

Throughout his career Albee has plotted the graph of man's attempt to relate to his social and metaphysical situation. His central belief is that expressed by Freud in *The Future of an Illusion*: "man cannot remain a child for ever; he must venture at last into the hostile world. This may be called *'education to reality'*." [2] From Peter's refusal to

1 Michael Rutenberg, *Edward Albee: Playwright in Protest* (New York: DBS Publications, 1969), p. 201.

2 Sigmund Freud, *The Future of an Illusion,* trans. W. D. Robson-Scott (London: Hogarth Press, 1928), p. 86.

acknowledge the simple inadequacy of his life in *The Zoo Story*, to George and Martha's illusory child in *Who's Afraid of Virginia Woolf?* and Julian's flight to religion in *Tiny Alice*, he has charted the desperate need for illusion which has afflicted society and left the individual trapped in permanent adolescence. Where Beckett sees man as irrevocably condemned to live out a metaphysical absurdity, Albee's position is basically existential. He sees the cataclysm as very much man's own creation and, as such, avoidable. This is the point of his comment, in the introduction to the published version of the plays that "A playwright—unless he is creating escapist romances (an honourable occupation, of course)—has two obligations: first, to make some statement about the condition of 'man' . . . and, second, to make some statement about the nature of the art form with which he is working. In both instances he must attempt change." [3]

He takes as his subject modern society's apparent determination to conspire in its own demise through a wilful refusal to risk the anguish which inevitably stems from personal commitment and from human relationships forged in an imperfect world. In the face of this the individual is urged to accept the realities which circumscribe and define his identity, while placing himself in implacable opposition to a social system which trades simple humanity for the dubious benefits of material success and an unruffled, if illusory, security. The movement which Albee detects towards fragmentation, in individual lives as in society at large, an anomie privately and publicly compensated for by a desperate commitment to any ordered structure (the longing for "law and order" is not without its metaphysical implications), is seen by him as a deadly flight from the saving grace of human interdebtedness. *Box* and *Quotations from Chairman Mao Tse-Tung* provide a focus for these earlier more random observations. In *Who's Afraid of Virginia Woolf?* he had suggested a political dimension to George and Martha's exorcism of illusion; in *Tiny Alice* he had detailed the origin and nature of religious delusion and in *A Delicate Balance* examined the social fictions deemed necessary to the continuance of corporate life. In his two experimental plays he attempts to bring together the whole meta-structure of illusions which together create the fabric of the private and public world, suspecting with Freud that, "having recognized religious doctrines to be illusions, we are at once confronted with the

[3] Edward Albee, *Box* and *Quotations from Chairman Mao Tse-Tung* (New York: 1970), p. 9. All future page references will be incorporated into the text.

further question: may not other cultural possessions, which we esteem highly and by which we let our life be ruled, be of a similar nature? Should not the assumptions that regulate our political institutions likewise be called illusions, and is it not the case that in our culture the relations between the sexes are disturbed by an erotic illusion, or by a series of erotic illusions." [4] This comprehensive network of illusion stretches even to those artists whose central objective opposes the ordered world of art to the frightening flux of reality. Where a writer like Wallace Stevens rejects Freud's assertion, seeing the poet as one "capable of resisting or evading the pressure of reality," giving to life "the supreme fictions without which we are unable to conceive of it," Albee embraces Freud's scepticism and sees the function of the writer as precipitating that "education to reality" which he had made the central tenet of *The Future of an Illusion.*

In *The Necessary Angel* Wallace Stevens observed that "the commonest idea of an imaginative object is something large. But apparently with the Japanese it is the other way round and with them the commonest idea of an imaginative object is something small. With the Hindu it appears to be something vermicular, with the Chinese, something round and with the Dutch, something square." [5] The remark could scarcely provide a more appropriate starting point to an analysis of *Box* and *Quotations from Chairman Mao Tse-Tung*—two plays which are not only structured around just such a "square" imaginative object but which examine the role and function of imagination, in the form of ideological constructs no less than artistic creations. For it was Stevens, too, who asserted that "the diffusion of communism exhibits imagination on its most momentous scale" following "the collapse of other beliefs," [6] thus establishing that very connection between the artist's "fictions" and social illusions which Albee was at pains to demonstrate.

The play opens on a stage dominated by a large cube—the sides picked out with masked spotlights. After five seconds we hear a voice come from the back or sides of the theatre—itself, of course, a box. The voice announces the subject, "Box," and then begins a monologue which is in fact the working out of a dialectic. The play is essentially the self-questioning voice of the artist or of any individual alive to per-

4 *Op. cit.,* p. 59.
5 Wallace Stevens, *The Necessary Angel* (London: Faber & Faber Ltd., 1960), p. 143.
6 *Ibid.*

sonal and public responsibilities. But the elegaic tone, together with re-iterated use of the past tense, makes it clear that this is both a prophecy and a post-apocalyptic elegy for a departed civilization; the play which follows offers an explanation for that cataclysm, a "memory of what we have not known," a memory "to be seen and proved later." (p. 27)

Box is a protest against the dangerously declining quality of life—a decline marked in one way by the corruption of genuine artistry to suit the demands of a consumer society which has no place for the artist except as a simple manufacturer, and in another by the growth of an amoral technology with a momentum and direction of its own: "system as conclusion, in the sense of method as an end, the dice so big you can hardly throw them any more." (p. 20) The growing sophistication of computer technology, the "advances" in military capacity, deprive the word "progress" of any real meaning. For now "progress is merely a direction, movement," (p. 21) which may mean nothing more than the ability to make "seven hundred million babies dead in the time it takes, took, to knead the dough to make a proper loaf." (p. 20) The final corruption lies in a fierce and total commitment to defend this system whatever the cost in human terms: "corrupt to the selfishness, to the corruption that we should die to keep it . . . go under rather than . . . killing all those children to make a point." (pp. 213–22)

In these circumstances art is in a dilemma. Either it reflects the dis-solution or it counterposes order to entropy. What is the role of art, in other words, in an age of crisis? Should the artist endorse social fictions or fly in the face of demands for a reassuring conformity? From one point of view, the voice admits, "the beauty of art is order—not what is familiar, necessarily, but order on its own terms . . . a billion birds at once, black net skimming the ocean . . . going straight . . . in a *direction*. Order!" But as we have seen the self-justifying progress of technology has both order and direction. What it lacks is precisely a moral dimension, the capacity for criticism. By this token, art becomes an anodyne: "the release of tension is the return to consonance." (p. 24) By implication the true artist must reject this comfortable social role. As Albee explained in an interview, the playwright is either "a manu-facturer who constructs entertainments for a buyer's market" or he is a social critic, a man whom he describes, significantly, as being "out-of-step with his society." The image is obviously close to that in *Box*. To Albee, it seems, the true man, like the true artist, opposes himself to the destructive errors of his society. The playwright is forced by his commitment to truth to produce a play which "should not have had to have been written," [7] to oppose the blind movement of the mass and move "fast in the opposite way" (p. 26) like the solitary bird who opposes his flight to that of the billion. If art has ceased celebrating human potential, if it stresses loss, dissolution, and corruption, to the point at which it seems to be obsessed with despair and the increasing difficulty of communication, it is because this is an accurate reflection of the age. Thus, it is logical enough that in such a period, as the voice laments, "art hurts." (p. 28) This is not, as some critics have suggested, a comment on the decline of art, but an honest image of a civilization blindly plunging towards extinction, clutching the while at chimeras in the sad misapprehension that order, precision, and competence constitute a valid alternative to simple humanity and honesty. To Albee, metaphysical purpose and order are credible only in the context of a delusory religious conviction, only, in other words, if everything can be regarded as "part of a . . . predetermination, or something that has already happened—in principle—well, under *those* conditions *any* chaos becomes order. Any chaos at all." (p. 71) Not believing in such an ineluctable destiny, he sees the individual as directly responsible for his own fate. The assertion of a reassuring determinism he finds insupportable. What is needed is a reassertion of humane values. In *Who's Afraid of Virginia Woolf?* Albee had tested the survival of American Revolutionary principles at mid-twentieth century. While he found them suffocated beneath an elaborate pattern of illusion and deception, exorcism was still a possibility. In *Box* apocalypse is simultaneously only a breath away and a historical fact on which the voice can remark, speaking from the grave or from the individual conscience of those half aware of disaster but still drawn to the consolation of public mythology or the final protection of solipsism.

Wallace Stevens has observed that "in an age in which disbelief is so profoundly prevalent or, if not disbelief, indifference to questions of belief, poetry and painting, and the arts in general, are, in their measure, a compensation for what has been lost." Man's interest "in the imagination and its work is to be regarded not as a phase of humanism but as a vital self-assertion in a world in which nothing but the self remains, if that remains." [8] This basic truth of modernism highlights the paradox of Albee's work. He has always been obsessed with a sense of loss—a theme which runs through his life as clearly as his plays—but he has also consistently refused to retreat into stoicism, which he

7 Rutenberg, *Edward Albee: Playwright in Protest*, p. 241.
8 Stevens, *The Necessary Angel*, p. 171.

regards as a cowardly and ultimately lethal retreat from commitment, or into protective illusion. As a writer he has shown a healthy scepticism towards the spurious products of the imagination, whether these take the form of O'Neill's pipe-dreams or the elaborate artifice of art. Yet his central theme—the need to reject the seductive consolation of unreality, the desperate necessity to abandon faith in a specious sense of order, and the urgency of genuine communication between individuals stripped of pretense and defensive posturing—is advanced in plays which are, of course, nothing more themselves than elaborate and carefully structured fictions in which invented characters act out a prepared and balanced scenario. His awareness of this dilemma is perhaps reflected in his ironical reference to the careful construction of the box, which stands as a persuasive analogue of the well-made play: "this is solid, perfect joins . . . good work . . . and so fastidious, like when they shined the bottom of the shoes . . . *and* the instep." (p. 19) Clearly these plays are in part an attempt to resolve such a dilemma. There are no characters in *Box*. *Quotations* borrows speeches from other writers and then fragments them until Albee's conscious control is to some degree subverted. Such structure as is apparent is supplied partly by chance, by random association, and by an audience for whom the box, which dominates the stage, becomes a *tabula rasa* to be interpreted variously as the artificial construction of an artist, a visual image of order, a paradigm of the theatre, an image of the restricted world in which the individual exists or the empty shell of the body whose voice lingers on as a warning and an epitaph.

In approaching these plays it is essential to recall Albee's comment that "the use of the unconscious in the twentieth-century theatre is its most interesting development" for we have his assurance that "whatever symbolic content there may be in *Box* and *Quotations from Chairman Mao Tse-Tung*, both plays deal with the unconscious, primarily." [9] Both works represent an experiment in liberating the dramatic event from the conscious and potentially restricting control of the writer. Similar experiments have been conducted with music by John Cage, though in pieces like "Rozart Mix" and "Williams Mix" he rigorously excluded all conscious control, in the one case surrendering the recording and composition to a number of other people, and in the latter, recording a collage of sounds by purely random means. Indeed he has subsequently rejected even this since it excluded that indeterminacy in

---

[9] Rutenberg, *Edward Albee: Playwright in Protest*, p. 247.

actual performance which he had come to value. Albee's practice, however, differs in several important respects, although, interestingly enough, he admits in the introduction to his diptych that he was attempting "several experiments having to do . . . in the main . . . with the application of musical form to dramatic structures." (p. 7) He insists on retaining for himself a tight control over rhythm and tone and establishes with considerable attention to detail the basic structure of the two plays. While he allowed chance to play an important role he also reserved the responsibility of manipulating the text to secure the maximum effect. Albee, moreover, is not retreating from the centrality of language in his work but is intent on discovering the potential of words freed from their immediate context and released from their function of forwarding the details of linear plot, delineating the minutiae of character, and establishing the context and structure of conscious communication. In *Box* the sibylline utterances of the disembodied voice, together with the enigmatic central image (in contrast to the allegorical directness of the central symbol in *Tiny Alice*), leave the audience to respond to intimations of personal loss and the suggestive outlines of a visual image on a sub-conscious and intuitive rather than a conscious and cerebral level. In *Quotations* coherent monologues are deliberately fragmented in order to release meaning, while private and public fears are juxtaposed according to chance assonance. The play is a collage of words and images; it uses surrealist methods not to reveal the marvellous but to penetrate the bland façade of modern reality—personal, religious, and political.

At first sight *Quotations* is a curious work. Of the four characters one is silent, one reads lines taken directly from Mao's quotations, one recites a poem written by the nineteenth-century popular poet Will Carleton, and only one speaks dialogue written by Albee himself (only slightly more than half of the lines were written by Albee). Like Breton with the printed word or Ernst with visual matter Albee is intent on bringing together disparate materials and experiences to create an image with the power to bypass intellectual evasion. Mao's quotations and Carleton's poems are to an extent simply "found" material with which he can create a play with the power to disturb not merely conventional notions of theatre—a discrete and highly structured model—but parallel assumptions about the nature of reality. The play is intended to capture not only the simultaneity of life—the complex interplay of public and private worlds—but also the fluid, evanescent, and equivocal quality of any art which sets out to plot the decline of morality and morale in an age bereft of convictions which genuinely touch the quick of life. With religion dead—the minister sits mute throughout the play—there is only political activism, a sentimental longing for lost innocence, the short-lived consolation of sexuality, or a deadly solipsism which hastens that cataclysm which is the inevitable product of such a massive failure of nerve.

Reverdy has said that "the image is a pure creation of the spirit. It cannot be born of a comparison but of the bringing together of two realities which are more or less remote. The more distant and just the relationship of these two conjoined realities, the stronger the image—the more evocative power and poetic reality it will have." [10] The "meaning" of *Quotations* lies in the interstices of the speeches, in the associations and ideas generated by the juxtaposition of seemingly unrelated experiences and interpretations of reality. The power which Albee finds in Mao's thoughts or Carleton's sentimental verses goes far beyond the tendentious banality of which each is equally capable. By placing their work in a totally different context, by allowing a fortuitous consonance of meaning to establish itself by the deliberate juxtaposition of passages which seem to comment on one another, he allows the play to generate its own meaning through association, implicit irony, and the careful modulation of tempo and tone. Albee sets the basic rules which the text must follow, rather as does Beckett in *Film* and Pinter in *Landscape*. He defines his characters' range of awareness and their degree of self-absorption. The play's effectiveness depends on the one hand on a minute observance of these rules, "alteration from the patterns I have set may be interesting, but I fear it will destroy the attempt of the experiment," (p. 36) and on the other on the range of meaning released by a willing acceptance of fortuitous assonances in the text. On one level at least it is an elaborate Rorschach test—an exercise in unconscious creation by the observer, though playwright and director shape the elaborate disjunctions as implicit meanings, ambiguities and rhythms become apparent. Sometimes the effect is bathetic, as in the following:

> *Chairman Mao.* . . . The commuinst ideological and social system alone is full of youth and vitality, sweeping the world with the momentum of an avalanche and the force of a thunderbolt.
> *Long-Winded Lady.* Exactly: plut!
>   (p. 44)

---

[10] Quoted in Patrick Waldberg, *Surrealism* (London: Thames and Hudson, 1965), p. 25.

sometimes sententiously serious:

> *Chairman Mao.* We must endeavor to establish normal diplomatic relations, on the basis of mutual respect for territorial integrity and sovereignty and of equality and mutual benefit, with all countries willing to live together with us in peace.
> *Long-Winded Lady.* It helps.   (pp. 55–56)

But, whatever the immediate effect, this interleaving of apparently remote realities not only provides a tenuous structure for the play but also indicates Albee's conviction that there is an ineluctable connection between the body and the body politic. The public dimension of private action, or, more usually, inaction, has always played a major role in Albee's work, from *The Zoo Story* through *Who's Afraid of Virginia Woolf?* and *Malcolm* to *A Delicate Balance.* Here the connection is forged less obliquely by the deliberate and repeated confrontation of the two levels of experience.

> *Chairman Mao.* From a long term point of view it is not the reactionaries but the people who are really powerful.
> *Voice, from Box.* Apathy, I think.
> *Chairman Mao.* . . . Was Hitler not overthrown? I also said that the czar of Russia, the emperor of China and Japanese imperialism were all paper tigers. As we know, they were all overthrown.
> *Long-Winded Lady.* All that falling.
> *Chairman Mao.* U.S. imperialism has not yet been overthrown and it has the atom bomb. I believe it also will be overthrown. It, too, is a paper tiger.
> *Long-Winded Lady.* And it became something of a joke. . . .   (pp. 63–65)

From one point of view the different characters represent past (Old Woman), present (Long-Winded Lady), and future (Mao); external, internal, and social reality. But Albee is less concerned with differences than with similarities. All are united in their insistence on the imperfections of life and their awareness of impending crisis. Despite the fact that the first production allowed Mao to step outside the restricted world of the box which dominates the stage, the play's stage directions seem to indicate that all the characters are in fact trapped within its confines, limited perhaps by their common humanity but more especially by their highly personal and rigid perceptions of reality. Mao and the Old Lady are conscious of the other characters but make no effort to communicate with them. The Long-Winded Lady and the

Minister have passed even beyond this, into solipsistic reverie or sullen non-involvement. Like the audience, which in part they represent, they are brought together briefly in a constricted environment, where they sit, uncommunicating, and reshape experience into maudlin entertainment, personal reminiscence, or political dogma.

The result is a play which rehearses some of the central fears of an age dominated by the prospect of nuclear annihilation—a play which expresses the fears of the individual trapped in a society which can no longer offer effective consolation for the imperfection of love and the inevitable movement towards personal extinction. Mao's homilies on the decline of imperialism chime surprisingly well with revelations of human cruelty and degeneration on an individual level, and here is a clue to Albee's strategy in a play which deliberately relates the inner world (the Long-Winded Lady's stream-of-consciousness narration) to the outer (Mao's political analysis of the role and nature of mankind). For the most part Albee quotes directly from Mao. He does, however, carefully omit a crucial section in one quotation, a section which offers some insight into his methodology. "The ideological and social system of capitalism," Mao asserts, resembles "a dying person who is sinking fast, like the sun setting beyond the western hills." [11] The drift towards a lonely and meaningless death by the Old Lady, and by the woman in Carleton's poem, together with the literal "sinking" of the Long-Winded Lady as she becomes increasingly aware of her mortality, have a persuasive relevance to the social system in which they function. The personal dimension is disintegrating. The Long-Winded Lady has lost her husband to the anarchic power of cancer; her daughter, separated from her husband, has no genuine feeling either for her or for those to whom she turns for consolation. The Old Woman recounts a story of the inhumanity which can lie in the family unit itself. The voice of *Box,* which now intrudes, points out the significance of all this, "It's the little things, the *small* cracks." (p. 75) The origins of national decline lie in the disintegration of personal relationships and the collapse of those values which provide the justification for personal survival. The naive and dangerous illusions propounded by Mao—"among the whites in the United States it is only the reactionary ruling circles who oppress the black people. . . . They can in no way represent the workers, farmers,

[11] Mao Tse-Tung, *Quotations from Chairman Mao Tse-Tung* (New York: Frederick A. Praeger, 1967), p. 13.

revolutionary intellectuals and other enlightened persons who comprise the overwhelming majority of the white people"—have their counterpart in the wilful and potentially fatal self-deceit of the Long-Winded Lady. It is not, as Michael Rutenberg suggests, a play about death; it is a play about dying—a distinction which the Long-Winded Lady is herself at pains to make. It is a description of the process which leads to the apocalypse implied by *Box,* which both precedes and follows it.

The play seems to take place outside of time, between the striking of the chord and its implicit resolution, the breaking of the bone and the pain, the dropping of the bomb and the "burning." It is a moment of truth in which the reasons for what seems an imminent disaster become simultaneously and belatedly apparent; as though we had "caught just the final instant, without time to relate the event to its environment—the thing happening to the thing happened *to*" (p. 50) but were dimly conscious of some causal relationship beneath the confusion. The play's method forces the audience into an attempt to reconstruct this meaning, not by re-assembling the shattered monologues but by relating them to each other in such a way as to become aware of the tenuous but real connections. If this process seems to lack clarity, it is worth recalling Breton's observation that lucidity is "the great enemy of revelation," for it is "only when the latter has come about that the former can be authorised to command respect for its rights." [12] As the Long-Winded Lady remarks, "if we control the unconscious, we're either mad or . . . dull-witted." (p. 60) Clarity of expression, linguistic precision, and coherent meaning are not synonymous with insight and genuine comprehension. Albee's suggestion that ours is a civilization which, like the individuals which it contains and which provide its direction and momentum, is in decline, "falling . . . by indirection," (p. 70) is not founded only on a rational analysis of political realities. It rests, more significantly, on an intuitive perception of the erosion of human values and on that retreat into the self which is both a denial of social life and a surrender of personal and public responsibility. It is this, it seems to Albee, which makes cruelty and even mutual annihilation an immediate possibility.

The withholding of an immediately available meaning creates an inevitable ambiguity, which serves to force the audience to supply

[12] Quoted in J. H. Matthews, *Surrealist Poetry in France* (Syracuse, N.Y., 1969), Syracuse University Press, p. 206.

specific reasons for a fear which the Long-Winded Lady refuses at first to specify. The result, one suspects, is that a trivial and even amusing incident becomes the means of expressing the unconscious and largely unexpressed neurosis of a generation. For, although the Long-Winded Lady is in fact describing her own plunge into the sea from the deck of an ocean liner, the audience, having listened to the post-holocaust monologue of *Box*, is likely to supply a more directly apocalyptic interpretation because "we do that . . . we make it happen a little before it need." (p. 50) When she wonders in retrospect what sound "it" must have made as "it" entered the water, having plummeted by amidst "the roar of the engines and the sea," the "thing . . . landing, and the spray, the sea, parting, as it were," the thought is paralleled in her mind by the memory of the carnage which followed a traffic accident and is juxtaposed to Mao's comment on the power of communism "sweeping the world with the momentum of an avalanche and the force of a thunderbolt." (p. 44) It is surely not fanciful to presume that in a nuclear age her enigmatic words should have overtones of cataclysm as she describes the successive stages of decline: "sun . . . haze . . . mist . . . deep night . . . all the spectrum down. Something. Burning" (p. 72) and asks, rhetorically, "how many are expecting it?" (p. 57) Her obsession with what she calls "all that falling" is in fact juxtaposed not only to the continuing story of the failure of human relationships, recited by the Old Lady, but also to Mao's brutally simplistic aphorisms on the atom bomb and the overthrow of American imperialism. Her description of the fall from the ship is indeed very like an account of the moment of annihilation itself, "suddenly, as sudden and sure as what you've always known and never quite admitted to yourself, it is not there; there is no railing, no wood, no metal, no buoy-life-thing saying S.S. or H.M.S. whatever, no . . . nothing! Nothing at all!" (p. 105)

In the introduction to the two plays Albee suggests that while they "are separate works" which "were conceived at different though not distant moments" and can "stand by themselves" and even be played separately, they are "more effectively performed enmeshed"; *Quotations*, indeed, being "an outgrowth of and extension of the shorter play." (p. 7) The connection between the two now seems clear enough. The drift towards death becomes most ominous precisely when one no longer has a clear perception of the value of life. Death comes by default as humane values are sacrificed to self-justification and political expediency. The kind of selfishness which enables a woman to respond to news of her husband's imminent death with the cry, "But what about *me!* Think about *me* . . . ME! WHAT ABOUT ME!" (p. 89) and which permits Mao to declare, "we are advocates of the abolition of war; we do not want war; but war can only be abolished through war," (p. 113) clearly threatens to destroy the very purpose of life itself.

In early performances *Quotations from Chairman Mao Tse-Tung* was followed by a complete reprise of *Box*. By degrees, however, the melancholy voice of *Box* was allowed to punctuate the painful revelations of the other play, providing both an additional counterpoint and a direct link between the two works. The intimations of corruption, the suggestions of impending apocalypse, which had opened and which now close the diptych stand explained. For this is a civilization which has wilfully blinded itself to the nature of reality and to the urgent need for some kind of spiritual renewal—a renewal which owes nothing to religion or to the secular substitute of political idealism. The play's implicit message is the necessity to re-establish the links between individuals which have been fractured by an instinctive self-interest and a perverse refusal to recognize man's imperfection. Mao's political optimism, his bland assurance (not included in the play but a recurrent theme of his actual speeches) that "the world is progressing, the future is bright and no one can change this general trend of history" [13] is as dangerously self-deluding as the Long-Winded Lady's denial of her introspection. Yet, as she recognizes, this process of self-deception is a familiar enough strategy: "one . . . concludes things —and if those things and what is really there don't . . . are not the *same* . . . well! . . . it would usually be better if it were so. The mind does that: it helps." (p. 55) But as Albee has consistently argued, such a denial of actuality, such an unwillingness to confront the sense of cruelty and loss which are an inescapable aspect of existence, is itself the prime cause of the drift towards isolation, despair and, ultimately, destruction. People no longer communicate because they inhabit separate worlds of their own construction and close their eyes to the entropic forces at work in their own lives as in society in general. Wallace Stevens may see the mind as "a violence from within that protects us from a violence without" or "the imagination pressing back against the pressure of reality" aiding "our self-preservation" and through "the sound of its words" helping "us to live our lives." But to Albee, such wilful deception merely compounds the "violence with-

---

[13] Mao Tse-Tung, *Quotations*, p. 38.

out" until the center can no longer hold. We are left at the end with a reprise of part of *Box*. That is, we are left with a stage completely empty except for the outlines of the box itself—a box which, with the exception of the dying tones of a voice finally settled into silence, is all that remains of the personal fear and public myth of an entire civilization.

Death Prattle

by Henry Hewes

The relative joylessness of modern life appears to be driving some of our foremost playwrights to abstraction. The latest instance is Edward Albee's *All Over,* in which an American Everywife awaits the death of her affluent and famous husband. Awaiting with her are "the other woman"; his middle-aged son and daughter; his best friend; an eighty-six-year-old doctor; and an elderly nurse. We never see the dying man, who is lying in a coma behind a hospital screen at the rear of the stage. Nor do we learn anything specific about him, for the playwright wants our attention on the other characters. The dying man is there is give them a reason to gather and to converse with more candor and emotion than usual, and to suggest that, with his passing, his satellites are moving into a fallow finality.

Because of the play's characters, its literary dialogue and its subject matter, one is immediately reminded of the late T. S. Eliot. But the differences between Eliot and Albee soon become apparent. It is not just that Eliot wrote verse that sounded like prose and that Albee writes prose that sounds like verse. It is the almost complete lack in *All Over* of the sense of nemesis that in Eliot's plays acted as a driving force against which the characters could struggle. Eliot believed in God and fate, and Albee, in this play at least, chooses not to. This choice is certainly appropriate to our times, and it makes *All Over* a realistic and honest effort to reflect contemporaneity. Yet, it leaves Albee with the difficult task of finding some other conflict that will be equally dramatic.

The obvious way to create such drama would be to find deeply revealing points of dispute between the characters. This would have been easy to do for none of them like one another very much and the wife is firmly opposed to complying with her husband's wish that he be cremated. Yet, again Albee has resisted. Why? One can only guess that he prefers to show us the overriding despair that reduces these people's lives to dispassion and makes their decisions unimportant.

Thus, *All Over* becomes a play of carefully orchestrated conversations in which recalled random thoughts and petty unresolved bickerings fill in a mosaic of waste. The husband presumably had a vital career, but those around him who used his wealth and supplied him with conventional satisfactions have diminished into stagnant, decaying people. Even his mistress seems unable to express the joy of her long relationship with him and instead recalls the ecstasy of a former love affair, which because of its brevity remains more perfect in memory.

The wife, on the other hand, can't remember falling in love with her husband. She repeats several times throughout the play, "Oh, God, the little girl I was when he came to me," and ultimately confesses that his appeal had been the serene security of being attached to an older man. Nevertheless, even though she briefly tried a sexual liaison with her husband's best friend, she knows she is incapable of loving anyone else. Both she and her husband's mistress foresee an unhappy old age without the man who has given their lives some meaning. That this meaning was made shabby for both of them is sad but is implied to be the legacy of a generation driven to indecisiveness by the breakdown of old traditions.

Would their lives have been less shabby if the husband had divorced his wife and married his mistress? Perhaps. But divorce is seen by the playwright as a kind of killing. Indeed, it is suggested that the threat of divorce was responsible for driving the best friend's wife to insanity. The subject is enlarged upon by the doctor's deliberations about the shift from Old Testament-inspired severity to New Testament-inspired mercy. The latter is more humane, but the older tradition may have produced a more vital Western civilization. Without advocating that all men with mistresses be cruel enough to divorce their wives, Albee has pointed out that indecisive living is an important factor in what many see as the decline of the West.

It is not just indecisiveness that is being criticized. *All Over* goes beyond that to examine the myth upon which the meaningfulness of marriage and love is based. In one of those characteristic Albee dissections of word distinctions, the mistress tells how she first became aware of "a faint shift from total engagement" in her affair with the husband, which led to a knowledge that all her sharing had been not "arbitrary" but "willful," and that nothing had been "inevitable or even necessary."

Existentialist philosophers may find glory in our ability to continue with such awareness, but in *All Over* the wife and mistress do little more than resign themselves to an insoluble unhappiness. In this respect, the play disappoints. Two hours of deathwatching would be more dramatic if they led to a release or a revitalization.

Also disappointing is the flatness of the other characters, about whom we never learn very much. The best friend is mousy. The son is a washout, whose response to his father's fame has been to become an uncompetitive timeserver. And the daughter, who has become involved with an opportunistic and unscrupulous married man, is cynical without being witty.

Director John Gielgud has apparently given the playwright the kind of production he wanted. There is a minimum of movement and color as the various characters speak more to the audience than to each other. Furthermore, although Rouben Ter-Arutunian's neutral setting of black velour and aluminum never distracts us from what the people are saying, it fails to supply a feeling of warmth and of being in a house where old tradition is passing.

Jessica Tandy brings a gracefulness of speech and manner to the role of the wife that noticeably exceeds the comparative tonelessness of most American performers. Colleen Dewhurst exhibits an understated inner strength as the mistress. And Betty Field is lively and forceful in two or three brief forays as the nurse.

However, it requires great effort on the audience's part to follow the quick shifts of dialogue and to appreciate some of Albee's set pieces of conversation that seem to lead the action nowhere. Because the emotional and intellectual rewards of doing this work are elusive, *All Over* commands our respect more as Albee's obstinately drawn abstraction of the state of things than it does as a dramatic work.

To the Brink of the Grave:
Edward Albee's *All Over*

by C. W. E. Bigsby

Throughout his work, Edward Albee has always been concerned with the failure of love to neutralize the pain of an existence which he thinks finally absurd if not redeemed by the integrity of human values. He has constantly flirted with apocalypse and has revealed a puritan conviction that the path to redemption lies through suffering. But he has repeatedly drawn back from the brink, sustained by a vision of liberal concern, by a conviction that it remains possible for individuals and, perhaps, nations, to be shocked into an awareness of the true nature of their situation and thus of the paramount need for compassion and, in the last resort, love, however imperfect that love may be.

With *Box* and *Quotations from Chairman Mao Tse-Tung*, that conviction seemed more attenuated and shrill. In his more recent play it genuinely seems *All Over*. For the basic process of human life appears to be structured on a slow withdrawal from the Other; a gradual plunge into the Self which must eventually result in spiritual collapse. Love itself seems nothing more than an expression of self-concern. As The Wife remarks, in what seems to be an accurate observation of the motives of those who surround her, "Selfless love? I don't think so; we love to *be* loved. . . . All we've *done* is think about ourselves. Ultimately." [1] This is as long a step from the self-sacrificing love of Jerry, in *The Zoo Story*, as the essentially static quality of his recent plays is from the exuberant action of his early work. The play ends, significantly, too significantly, with the words, "All over."

The tone in his recent plays is, then, no longer that of a confident

[1] Edward Albee, *All Over* (London, 1972), p. 109. All subsequent page references will be incorporated in the text.

liberalism rehearsing the great verities of the nineteenth century—personal and public responsibility. As The Mistress remarks, the only way "we keep the nineteenth century going for ourselves" is to "pretend it exists." (p. 36) The tone now is elegaic. The rhythm is no longer the vibrant crescendo and diminuendo of *Who's Afraid of Virginia Woolf?* and *Tiny Alice*. It is the slow, measured, and finally faltering pulse beat of *Box* and *Quotations from Chairman Mao Tse-Tung*.

Yet, Albee's concern in *All Over* is essentially that of his earlier work. He remains intent on penetrating the bland urbanities of social life in an attempt to identify the crucial failure of nerve which has brought individual men and whole societies to the point not merely of soulless anomie but even of apocalypse. In *The Zoo Story* he had indicted a retreat into the self which was an escape both from responsibility and personal involvement; a state of mind in which the fantasies conjured up by pornographic playing cards are accepted as a legitimate substitute for reality. In *Who's Afraid of Virginia Woolf?* fiction is seen as a desperate and finally destructive strategy adopted by those for whom the world is fraught with pain and complexity. In *All Over* Albee pursues this flight from reality to its source in personal betrayal, to a flaw in human character which must be faced if it is to be understood and remedied. His subject is, in the words of The Mistress, "the tiniest betrayal—nothing so calamitous as a lie held on to in the face of fact, or so niggling as a fantasy during the act of love, but in between—and it can be anything, or nearly nothing, except that it moves you back into yourself a little." (16)

The play gathers together a group of people whose lives have in various ways been intertwined. They have come to witness the death of a man whose important role in public affairs provides the link, ever-present in Albee's mind, between private and public failure. The moment is one which would seem to demand the truth; it is an occasion for summaries and confessions and these we are offered as Albee draws together the threads of deceit and pain and treachery which provide the real bonds between those who should be linked by love and compassion.

The compelling power of death, Albee observes, is, after all, not that it inspires sympathy for the dying but that, for a moment, before we control and neutralize it with ceremony, it turns us back into ourselves to face our own vulnerability and hence, perhaps, to confess our guilt and weaknesses. Yet, if it can dislodge truth from its conventional concealment it can also underline a fundamental selfishness as we view the death purely in terms of its impact upon ourselves. As The Wife recognizes in a crucial speech, "All we've done . . . is think about ourselves. There's no hope for the dying. I suppose. Oh my; the burden . . . What will become of *me* . . . and *me* . . . and *me*." (109)

The man who is dying and who we never see is, effectively, an abstraction. He lies behind a screen which, while functional, is also, to Albee, an appropriate image of the determination with which we protect ourselves from the central fact of human existence, namely the arbitrary and ineluctable nature of its termination. For the implication of such a fact is plainly either that derived by the absurdist or that offered by the humanist, for Albee permits no evasive flirtation with religion. Yet, while instinctively opposed to the constrictive determinism of the absurdist, he observes the wilful persistence with which people fail to accept the obligations laid on them by a life which generates no meaning and no consolation of itself. His world has been littered with solitary individuals who have fought to protect their solitude, failing to recognize that what Jerry calls "solitary free passage," in *The Zoo Story*, is not gain but "further loss." [2] In *All Over* the characters respond to the painful details of terminal illness, with its literally bloody details (at one stage a hemorrhage splatters the nurse's uniform), with callous self-concern. The man's son and daughter are caught in their own psychic dramas which are, in turn, an expression of the failure of love in their family. His best friend has in the past committed adultery and has thereby perhaps contributed to his own wife's insanity. Indeed, the crucial deaths in *All Over* have all happened before the play begins, before the illness which strikes down the unseen character. For Albee's real subject is the collapse of the spirit, the slow extinction of those human qualities which might be used to counter the natural absurdity of man's condition.

Nor are the deaths about which he speaks simply the slow suicides of those who cut themselves off from other people. For he is equally concerned with murder—not merely the brutal lack of compassion which makes physical murder possible but the conscious and deliberate maiming of the spirit of those whose emotional commitment makes them especially vulnerable. As The Wife observes, there is a sense in which divorce is an act of murder, as are all the individual acts of betrayal, greed, and self-interest. The process of living thus becomes no more than a matter of learning to protect oneself from other people,

2 Edward Albee, *The American Dream and The Zoo Story* (New York, 1963) p. 35.

learning to distrust words and suppress an emotional openness which may simply make one vulnerable. And the consequence is a slow diminution of humanity. The Wife comments, "You make a lot of adjustments over the years, if only to avoid being eaten away. Anger, resentment, loss, self-pity—*and* self-loathing—loneliness. You can't live with all that in the consciousness very long, so, you put it under or it gets well, and you're never sure which. Worst might be if there's nothing there any more, if everything has been accepted," (102) for not only does this lead to a situation in which, as she confesses, "I don't love *anyone* . . . Any more" (103) but it destroys the capacity to express genuine feeling. As The Mistress asks, "What words will you ever have left if you use them all to kill? What words will you summon up when the day *comes*, as it may, poor you, when you suddenly discover that you've been in love?" (64)

But here, once again, is ample evidence that Albee is not an absurdist. The absurdity which he identifies is a wilful product of man, not the casual gift of an indifferent universe. He peoples his plays, not with the cosmic victims of Samuel Beckett, but with the self-created victims of modern society. The irony of Beckett's plays lies in the failure of his characters to recognize that things cannot be other than they are; the irony of Albee's plays lies in the failure of his characters to realize that things can be other than they are. At the same time this does not make him a confident social critic with a political blueprint for a future society. It is simply that he asserts a potential for action and concedes the existence of human values in a way which would be alien to the absurdist. The values that he endorses are essentially liberal ones, but this is a liberalism fully aware of the human and social realities which have made the absurdist vision such a compelling feature of the post-war world. For, of course, a writer whose solution to a contemporary sense of anomie is love, risks a potentially disabling sentimentality. Although he is not guilty of the confusion between Eros and Agape—which distorts and all too often trivializes a similar theme in the work of Tennessee Williams and James Baldwin—in placing the weight of his liberal commitment squarely on man's potential for selfless compassion he is in danger of simplifying human nature and falsifying the history of personal and social relations. It is his considerable achievement that for the most part he successfully avoids the trap. If he calls for a renewal of human contact and a resolute acceptance of the real world, he is prepared to concede the tenuous nature of his solution and the increasingly desperate nature of personal and social reality. The liberal values which he embraces are indeed associated in *All Over* with a generation approaching death. The point is clear. Modern society has replaced human relationships with pragmatic alliances, and the values which used to sustain the social structure are at risk. The society which he pictures is flirting with its own extinction, as one character suggests that condemned prisoners wish to embrace their executioner.

The difficulty of such an assumption, however, is that it implies a romantic nostalgia for an unexamined past. Throughout his work Albee has made appeals to the values of a former age, through the person of Grandma in *The American Dream* and *The Sandbox*, George the historian, in *Who's Afraid of Virginia Woolf?*, and the aging Tobias in *A Delicate Balance*, without ever questioning the reality of those values or their historical force. The immediate future, on the other hand, is represented by a series of caricatures. The Young Man in *The American Dream* and *The Sandbox*, Nick in *Who's Afraid of Virginia Woolf?*, Claire in *A Delicate Balance*, and The Son in *All Over* are all vacuous, impotent, sterile, or sexually incomplete. It is a terminal generation with no apparent understanding of vital human needs.

His real concern is with the generation which has shaped the moral environment which such people will inherit. For people like George and Tobias, the inheritors of a liberal tradition and instinctive humanists, have allowed themselves to be cowed by the pressures of modern existence. They have capitulated to the aggressive Caesarism of the age and as a result have bequeathed only their own nerveless incapacity to the next generation. The essential drama of most of Albee's plays lies in the battle of these vaccilating liberals to lay claim to the values which they had so casually deserted. *All Over* rests on an entropic vocabulary: "winding down," "withdrawal," "diminishing," "abandonment," "spinning back," "dying." Time is running out, not only for the dying man but for a dying civilization. The references to the assassination of the Kennedys and of Martin Luther King are intended to project the implications of the play beyond the confines of a single deathbed. The connection he seeks is that between the body and the body politic, as society reflects the dissolution, the failure of human relationships, the abandonment of responsibility and the callous indifference, observable on an individual scale. He is concerned with a society whose social forms would seem to indicate a New Testament compassion but whose private convictions are rooted in Old

World brutality. As one character laments, "What a sad and shabby time we live in." (42) For a civilization which regards the daily realities of life as merely "a way of getting through from ten to six," (60) as a way of avoiding metaphysical questions of a kind which may threaten even at "the sight of one unexpected, ludicrous thing," (83) clearly stands in risk of collapse. And the New Testament love, which Albee has preached from *The Zoo Story* onwards, a love defined in *All Over* by The Mistress as "love with mercy . . . the kind you can't hold back as a reward, or use as any sort of weapon," (64) fails because of an egotism which is not even self-love but rather a self-mocking suppression of all feelings. That two characters in *All Over* do continue to insist on the reality of selfless love, despite their own many failures, is a ground for hope. That they are, respectively, sixty-one and seventy-one years old reveals the imminence of that private and public apocalypse which Albee has been prophesying and fighting throughout his work.

The real problem of *All Over* is that Albee seems here to succumb to a basic conviction of American theatre, namely that seriousness and pretentiousness are in some way necessarily allied. To all intents and purposes *All Over* is Albee's version of Arthur Miller's *After the Fall*. There is the same concern with human failure and betrayal, the same anguished fascination with the slow decay of love which mirrors the physical slide towards the grave. His characters speak the same pseudo-poetic prose, creating a ceremony of death which is part expiation and part celebration. There is also, alas, the same sacrifice of language and theatrical truth to a deeply felt personal anguish, so that the result is a play which paradoxically fails to create anything more compelling than imitation baroque—verbal arabesques, and emotional arpeggios rooted in no recognizable human sensibility. The play is not realistic. Albee's drawing rooms, like Pinter's, are charged with metaphysics; they glow with significance. Sometimes, as in Albee's *Who's Afraid of Virginia Woolf?* or Pinter's *The Birthday Party*, realism and symbolism blend into powerful metaphor; sometimes, as in *All Over* or *Old Times*, the metaphor crushes the characters until one admires tone, tempo, rhythm, register, imagery, everything but human relevance. And that price is especially great in Albee's work where he is intent on urging precisely the need for such relevance. Albee seems to have placed himself in the paradoxical position of stressing the need for a revival of liberal values in a play with no recognizable human beings. An expressionistic satire such as *The American Dream* can bear such an approach, though even here Grandma's subversive vitality is a crucial element in emphasizing the survival of non-utilitarian standards. In *All Over* the paradox is potentially destructive. Albee has come more and more to resemble T. S. Eliot in creating didactic ceremonies, cerebral puppet shows manipulated with an impressive economy of energy, but dangerously lacking in the kind of compelling humanity and subtle theatricality which makes Beckett's work, for example, so much more than an intellectual valedictory.

Chronology of Important Dates

1928   Born March 12th. Adopted by millionaire Reed Albee and his wife, Frances.

1940   Lawrenceville School. Wrote a juvenile play, *Aliqueen*.

1943   Dismissed from Lawrenceville and sent to Valley Forge Military Academy. Subsequently dismissed.

1944   Goes to Choate School where he begins to write.

1945   First published work, a poem entitled, "Eighteen," published in *Kaleidograph*.

1946   First published play, "Schism," appeared in the *Choate Literary Magazine*. He also wrote a novel and a considerable amount of poetry. Moves to Trinity College, Hartford, Connecticut where he played the role of Emperor Franz Joseph in Maxwell Anderson's *The Masque of Kings*.

1947   Leaves college and writes continuity material for music programs on WNYC radio.

1948–1958   Lives in Greenwich Village and works as an office boy for an advertising agency, as a salesman in the record department at Bloomingdale's, as an assistant in Gimbel's book department, as a barman in the Manhattan Towers Hotel, and as Western Union messenger. In 1958, in the space of three weeks, he wrote *The Zoo Story*.

1959   The first production of *The Zoo Story*, at the Schiller Theater Werkstatt, Berlin, September 28.

1960   The first American production of *The Zoo Story*, at the Provincetown Playhouse. *The Death of Bessie Smith* is produced at the Schlosspark Theater, Berlin, April 21. *The Sandbox* produced at The Jazz Gallery, New York, April 15. *Fam and Yam* produced at The White Barn, Westport, Connecticut, August 27.

1961   *The American Dream* produced at the York Playhouse, New York, January 24. *Bartleby,* an opera based on Melville's short story, written in collaboration with William Flanagan, is poorly received and withdrawn.

1962   *Who's Afraid of Virginia Woolf?,* Billy Rose Theatre, New York, October 13. Nominated for Pulitzer Prize. Nomination not accepted by full committee and two members of drama sub-committee resign. Received New York Drama Critics Award and Tony Award.

1963   *The Ballad of the Sad Café,* Martin Beck Theatre, New York, October 20.

1964   *Tiny Alice,* Billy Rose Theatre, December 29.

1966   *Malcolm,* Schubert Theatre, New York, January 11. The play was a commercial failure and closed after five days. *A Delicate Balance,* Martin Beck Theatre, New York, September 22. Received the Pulitzer Prize.

1967   *Everything in the Garden,* an adaptation of a play by Giles Cooper, opened at the Plymouth Theatre, New York, November 16.

1968   *Box* and *Quotations from Chairman Mao Tse-Tung,* Buffalo Studio Arena Theatre, March 7.

1971   *All Over,* Martin Beck Theatre, New York, March 27.

1975   *Seascape,* New York, January 23.

Notes on the Editor and Contributors

C. W. E. BIGSBY, Senior Lecturer in American Literature at the University of East Anglia, is the author of a study of contemporary American drama entitled *Confrontation and Commitment* and a monograph on Edward Albee. He is also the author of *Dada and Surrealism* and has edited a collection of essays under the title *The Black American Writer* and another under the title *Superculture: The Influence of American Popular Culture on Europe.*

ROBERT BRUSTEIN, Dean of the Yale Drama School, is theatre reviewer for the *New Republic.* He is the author of *The Theatre of Revolt* and has collected his reviews and critical essays in *Seasons of Discontent, The Third Theatre,* and *Theatre as Revolution.*

HAROLD CLURMAN, critic and director, is the author of *The Fervent Years,* the story of the Group Theatre which he founded in association with Lee Strasberg. He has also collected his reviews and critical essays in *Lies Like Truth* and *The Naked Image.*

GILBERT DEBUSSCHER, a university lecturer in Belgium, is the author of the first study of Albee's work, *Edward Albee: Tradition and Renewal.* He is presently the Chairman of the Belgium/Luxembourg Association for American Studies.

MARTIN ESSLIN, the head of Drama for BBC radio, is the author of *Brecht: The Man and His Work; The Theatre of the Absurd; Reflections: Essays on Modern Theatre;* and *The Peopled Wound: The Plays of Harold Pinter.* He is also a former visiting professor at Florida State University and has been a visiting lecturer at the Salzburg Seminar.

ABRAHAM N. FRANZBLAU is a psychiatrist who practices in New York City.

JOHN GIELGUD is a distinguished actor famous for his work in both contemporary and Shakespearean drama. He is also a director and was responsible for the New York production of Albee's *All Over.*

HENRY HEWES, drama reviewer of the *Saturday Review,* is a former faculty member of the Salzburg Seminar. He is the editor of *Famous Plays of the 1940's* and *The Best Plays of 1961–2, 1962–3, 1963–4.*

ANNE PAOLUCCI, Research Professor at St. John's University in Jamaica, New York, and editor of *The Review of National Literatures,* is the author of

A Short History of American Drama, Classical Influences in Shakespearean Tragedy and *From Tension to Tonic: The Plays of Edward Albee*.

PHILIP ROTH, author and critic, has published a number of novels and short story collections, including *Goodbye Columbus, Letting Go, When She Was Good, Portnoy's Complaint,* and *Our Gang.* His stories have appeared in *The New Yorker, Esquire, Commentary,* and the *Paris Review.*

MICHAEL E. RUTENBERG, Associate Professor of Theatre at Hunter College in New York City, is the author of *Edward Albee: Playwright in Protest.*

RICHARD SCHECHNER, former editor of *Tulane Drama Review,* is a theatre director, working with his own group of actors, The Performance Group. He is the author of many articles on theatre and of a study of the Free Southern Theatre.

ALAN SCHNEIDER, an American director, was responsible for the first American productions of the work of Beckett, Pinter, and Albee. He has directed both on and off Broadway and is a former faculty member of the Salzburg Seminar.

R. S. STEWART was formerly a staff member of *The Atlantic Monthly.*

DIANA TRILLING, essayist and editor, is the author of *Claremont Essays,* and editor of *The Viking Portable D. H. Lawrence, Selected Letters of D. H. Lawrence,* and *Huckleberry Finn.*

BRIAN WAY, Senior Lecturer in American Literature at the University College of Wales, Swansea, is the author of many articles on American literature.

GERALD WEALES, Professor of Drama at the University of Pennsylvania, has published theatre reviews in *Commonweal, The Reporter,* and *Drama Survey.* He is the author of several books, including *American Drama Since World War II, Religion in Modern English Drama,* and *The Jumping-Off Place: American Drama in the 1960's.*

ROSE A. ZIMBARDO, Professor of English at the State University of New York, Stonybrook, is the author of many articles on drama.

Selected Bibliography

Amacher, Richard. *Edward Albee.* (New York: Twayne Publishers, 1969).

Baxandall, Lee. "The Theatre of Edward Albee," *Tulane Drama Review,* IX, iv (1965), 19–40.

Bigsby, C. W. E. *Confrontation and Commitment: A Study of Contemporary American Drama.* (Columbus: University of Missouri Press, 1969).

————. *Albee.* (Edinburgh: Oliver and Boyd Ltd., 1969).

Cohn, Ruby. *Edward Albee.* (Minneapolis: Minnesota University Press, 1969).

Debusscher, Gilbert. *Edward Albee: Tradition and Renewal,* trans. Mrs. Anne D. Williams. (Brussels: American Studies Centre, 1967).

Diehl, Digby. "Edward Albee Interviewed," *Transatlantic Review,* XIII (Summer, 1963), 57–72.

Downer, Alan S., ed. "An Interview with Edward Albee," in *The American Theatre.* (Washington: U.S.I.S., 1967).

Flanagan, William. "The Art of the Theatre IV: Edward Albee," *The Paris Review,* XXXIX (Fall, 1966), 92–121. Reprinted in *Writers at Work.* (New York: Viking, 1967).

Harris, Wendell V. "Morality, Absurdity, and Albee," *Southwest Review,* XLIX (Summer, 1964), 249–256.

Kerjan, Liliane. *Albee.* (Paris: Seghers, 1971).

Lee, A. Robert. "Illusion and Betrayal: Edward Albee's Theatre," *Studies,* LIX (Spring, 1970), 53–67.

Lewis, Allan. "The Fun and Games of Edward Albee," *Educational Theatre Journal,* XVI (1964), 29–39. Reprinted in *Plays and Playwrights of the Contemporary Theatre.* (New York: Crown Publishers, Inc.).

Markus, Thomas B. "*Tiny Alice* and Tragic Catharsis," *Educational Theatre Journal,* XVII (October, 1965), 225–233.

Miller, Jordan. "Myth and the American Dream: O'Neill to Albee," *Modern Drama,* VII, i (September, 1964), 190–198.

Paolucci, Anne. *From Tension to Tonic: The Plays of Edward Albee.* (Carbondale: Southern Illinois University Press, 1972).

Phillips, Elizabeth C. "Albee and the Theatre of the Absurd," *Tennessee Studies in Literature,* X (1965), 73–80.

Post, Robert M. "Fear Itself: Edward Albee's *A Delicate Balance,*" *College English Association Journal,* XIII (1969), 163–171.

Rule, Margaret W. "An Edward Albee Bibliography," *Twentieth Century Literature,* XIV (April, 1968), 35–45.

Rutenberg, Michael E. *Edward Albee: Playwright in Protest* (New York: Avon, 1969).

Samuels, Charles Thomas. "The Theatre of Edward Albee," *Massachusetts Review,* VI (Autumn–Winter 1964–5), 187–201.

Willeford, William. "The Mouse in the Model," *Modern Drama,* XII (September, 1969), 135–145.

Witherington, Paul. "Albee's Gothic: The Resonances of Cliche," *Comparative Drama,* IV, 151–165.

Wolfe, Peter. "The Social Theatre of Edward Albee," *Prairie Schooner,* XXXIX, iii (Fall, 1965), 248–262.